# Growing Leadership

# Growing Leadership

✦

## Managing Developmental Chaos

*Glenn Jackson*

iUniverse, Inc.
New York  Bloomington  Shanghai

# Growing Leadership
## Managing Developmental Chaos

iUniverse books may be ordered through booksellers or by contacting:

iUniverse
1663 Liberty Drive
Bloomington, IN 47403
www.iuniverse.com
1-800-Authors (1-800-288-4677)

Because of the dynamic nature of the Internet, any Web addresses or links contained in this book may have changed since publication and may no longer be valid.

The views expressed in this work are solely those of the author and do not necessarily reflect the views of the publisher, and the publisher hereby disclaims any responsibility for them.

ISBN: 978-0-595-50603-3 (pbk)
ISBN: 978-0-595-49942-7 (cloth)
ISBN: 978-0-595-61577-3 (ebk)

Printed in the United States of America

# *Contents*

"As a leader, you need to ensure your followers believe in their ability to succeed. You must provide situations, training, coaching and experiences for them that allow them to experience success. Otherwise, you are giving them mediocrity and expecting them to rise to excellence by themselves. This is an unfair position for anyone."

"It is possible to motivate people for a short time externally through fear, high reward or some other out of the ordinary device; but true motivation for all individuals is internal."

"As the leader, you must know what everyone is doing without being intrusive of his or her work. You must know if someone is operating below potential, at maximum capacity or overload. You must know the morale and climate of the culture of the organization and smaller teams. You must know the business threats and opportunities, as well as internal strengths and weaknesses. In short, you must have extensive situational awareness at all times in order to be effective."

"People tend to relax after they perceive they have proven themselves. The problem with this is the act of relaxation is, in truth, a lowering of standards. Whatever you tolerate becomes the standard. For this reason, leadership demands you only tolerate behavior and performance that exist with high expectations."

"Leadership is not a day job. It is a "full engagement lifestyle," that takes a large part of your time and energy. This level of leadership commitment requires a selfless approach to your time and energy. You gain responsibility for development, coaching, discipline, performance and success for a team or organization. Anything less than your all to ensure this success is selling your commitment short and selling those who now depend on you short."

"A leader that has no vision will lead an organization to that end. An organization that does not know where it wishes to go will get there. The problem in both of these statements is that the destination achieved probably will not be exactly where it should be. Nevertheless, even if no one provides a vision, the organization will still go somewhere."

"There are many situations that do not neatly fall into the general development categories we have discussed. For that reason, I have added some specific conversations about some specific items you need to consider and think about."

"The guiding principal I have used for tool development is quite simple–it must be thorough, skill focused and applied evenly."

"Lastly, being the best you can be, in regards to developing your character and ability, is the right thing to do for personal development and growth. We all get older. Not everyone gets older while experiencing the depth of value that can be found from true ownership of their person, their time and their relationships. You have that power."

# *Introduction*

My working life has been spent trying to understand why people do what they do. I have constantly observed and studied human behavior from a leadership development and application perspective.

It interests me to observe how leaders behave and to observe the impact of their leadership behaviors. It generates a multitude of questions, both external and internal.

How do you grow leadership? Or should you ask, "How do I grow into leadership?" They are both interesting questions with no clear or easily defined answer. Essentially, this is why I wrote this book. I wanted to express in a personal dialogue, things I have learned along the way to help provide some tools others could use in their personal journey.

There are two things to remember as you read this book. First, the qualities, skills and characteristics discussed in this book are applicable to organizational leadership development. Second, and of even greater importance to me, is that these same characteristics and skills are applicable in your personal development, as you grow in life. After all, before you can ever lead or manage others successfully, you have to learn to lead and manage your self.

In my career I have participated in many organizational processes designed to develop leaders. I served in the US Air Force for 25 years and experienced an excellent leadership development process. I have also experienced leadership development and applied the processes learned from several business organizations. I wrote this book to talk about the lessons I have learned through participation in all of these processes. Why process? Quite simply, everything functions within a process of some sort. Things begin and end; develop and change; get better or worse. Human development falls within the same context.

What truly interests me is how and why we do what we do. And of even greater interest to me is how we develop supervisors from workers. These individuals will be further developed into managers and leaders at the lowest levels of organization that support the upper level leaders' vision, and then transition them into senior leaders, so getting it right the first time is critical for future organizational success.

I have observed leaders that made me sick, and I have observed leaders that truly inspired. I always asked myself–what do these extremes have in common?

The answer is simple–they are the result of the process that developed them into who they were. I am not discounting personality as a leading indicator of leadership. An individual's personality must be considered to have a huge influence on the type of leader she develops into. However, absent a process that coaches, mentors and develops positive personality aspects while working to reduce negative personality aspects, personality becomes the central leadership characteristic. This is not necessarily the best option.

To address this we have to look at the actual process we put people through in their development stages. Once someone has many years of experience in a leadership role it is hard to change them. That is why the best place to start is at the entry level position. Then the idea of change can be embedded within someone and they will take positive coaching and mentoring in a manner designed to continuously develop in a positive manner.

I worked for a Lieutenant Colonel in the US Air Force who truly inspired me. He led by example, set the tone, coached, felt the pain of others, worked hard, rewarded good performance, quietly coached poor performance to improve, and was loved by his troops.

I worked for a CEO who drove everyone to distraction, made promises he did not keep, constantly pushed without giving back and generally reduced the morale of his team.

Why could not the second example, the CEO, understand the negative impact of his choices and realize his was empty leadership? Why did the first example, the Lieutenant Colonel, so ably live the very truth of leadership, apparently so effortlessly?

These questions summarize the issue of process. What processes did these individuals undergo that resulted in the behaviors of leadership they demonstrated? Can someone be mentored or coached into leadership excellence? Is there not a process wherein the emergent follower exemplifies leadership?

Over the years, I have questioned, thought, experimented and strove to understand leadership, human nature, and psychology; whatever you want to call it– the core of demonstrated behavior that is leadership. I have read, observed and attempted to recreate situations where various development models would yield fairly good determined results.

This book is as much about my journey to understanding the forces that create leadership as it is about leadership itself. I hope you enjoy it. I believe you will gain insight from it. I know that when this process is implemented it yields positive results, because it has for me.

A few comments before proceeding:

- A leader without followers is not a leader.

- A leader who has incompetent or inept followers leads a rabble.

- Only a leader who leads effective, committed and competent followers can be said to truly lead.

- All leaders are followers.

- Leadership cannot exist without followers.

- Leadership does not exist without ownership.

- Followership does not exist without leadership skill and ownership energy.

- Leadership application starts at the bottom, not at the top.

- The most significant ingredient in transcending followership to leadership is ownership.

Throughout this book there will be multiple references to leadership, ownership and followership. These three concepts are inter-related and inseparable from each other. Every skill or value discussed is part of all three of these concepts. However, the main focus of the process deals with entry as a follower, learning and growing to become an owner, and finally stepping out to become a leader.

# 1

## *Courage*

One of the most interesting things to do, in organizing this book, was to decide where to start. As I thought about all the things you have to learn or do to understand leadership development, I started to think about the one thing that provides support for it all. I discovered that the single underlying difference between someone who proactively behaves versus someone who reactively behaves is the courage to act. So I begin this book about growing leadership with some comments about courage.

One thing I discovered a long time ago is that leadership is not always fun. There is a tremendous amount of work you must do and sacrifices you must make in order to be a leader. So just remember that while this entire process is extremely rewarding, it is not easy.

The same can be said for developing leadership qualities within your self. If you think it is easy to exert the willpower necessary to change your self, you are mistaken. And if you think that changing your self in a way that is contrary to your friends or associates is easy, think again; because it is not easy. It takes courage.

Depending on where you are in life, you are possibly setting out on a path of employment as a working person, completing your education for academic knowledge, pursuing self-discovery as a new supervisor, managing an extensive business process as a leader, or just trying to find a path to improve your own life and the lives of those around you. In all cases, there are challenges.

I cannot remember a time when any position I held did not have its own share of challenges. Every position, regardless of the level of complexity, has challenges. Every position has opportunities. Every position enables you to grow in some manner.

Learning, growing and celebrating success is fun. Helping others grow and seeing that success is fun. Leading a team and seeing them succeed is fun. Nevertheless, some aspects of the leadership role are not necessarily enjoyable. And yet, facing the challenges head-on and doing it with character is intrinsically one of the most rewarding and exhilarating experiences you will have. It validates you as a competent person with character.

But let's face it, taking on the responsibility for the work of others can be hard. Having to discipline someone can be hard. Keeping your personal feelings and attitudes out of the process and seeing things through someone else's perspective is hard. And sometimes the solutions you must bring to the table can be painful–so this too can be hard.

Take for example the setting in which you are assigned your first team. How scary is it to know that you're future rides on your team's performance, your organizations performance rides on your team's performance, and your team's performance rides on your ability to provide all the support, guidance and direction they need to be successful? If that does not cause you to stop and think about the scary side of performance—failure, I don't know what would.

Fear of failure is one of the biggest fears all of us must face. No individual on a team performs in an excellent manner at all times. When the negative cycle hits your team in unison and they are almost all having a bad day (as it will at some point) they just don't perform as they should–and you get the heat for it—that is not fun. These are the challenging times when your character and all your skills are truly tested.

This is when you get to show courage. Courage is more than the individual pieces defined below. Courage is the ability to reach down inside of your self and find the strength to forge ahead. The best definition I have ever heard of courage is this:

### Courage is action in the face of fear.

Many things give us fear. As I said above, fear of failure is one of the worst. Each of us feels fear in different ways over different things. However, we all share the basic requirement to face our fear and act. That is courage.

Courage is necessary for many reasons in the growth process. But fundamentally, if you are afraid to try, you will not grow. In order to be able to try, you have to overcome your fear of failure, or looking silly, or any other perceptions you have. In short, you must demonstrate courage to yourself. That is the starting point.

*I had one of the lead roles in a musical when I was in high school. I was Curly in Oklahoma. I do not know how to describe the feeling, or the rush, of walking out on stage, dressed in a costume and makeup, singing "Oh What A Beautiful Day," with an audience of a thousand in attendance.*

*Talk about an opportunity to learn courage! Acting in front of people builds your sense of self confidence. Self confidence is necessary to generate the courage necessary to overcome the fear of failing or doing something really stupid in front of people.*

I know this experience helped me when I had to give my first speech. I had already been through the feeling of being in front of people. I had found my way to overcome that fear and perform. Giving a speech was much the same. I demonstrated courage.

Taking a team of people on a mission as the leader also requires courage. You must have self confidence and believe you can do it. Then you do. You face your fear and overcome it. This is courage.

Courage is a basic ability or skill each leader must master. It takes courage to speak in front of a group. It takes courage to present new ideas or take a position that varies from the group. It takes courage to separate yourself from the group when you first step into a supervisory position.

- You know what scares you. When you feel that fear, take the time to evaluate it.

- Take it apart and analyze it. What is it, specifically, that is creating your fear?

- Identify it. Look at ways you can address a part of it.

- Think about how you can overcome it.

- Visualize how you have seen other leaders behave in a similar situation.

- Then try and emulate that behavior. Try and beat it. Work at it.

Courage is an inner strength that will sustain you in the long drive toward self improvement and career progression. Courage will give you the strength to stand out in the crowd, be different, noticed and lead.

- A Different Perspective or Better Idea

In the natural progression of growth, there comes a time when you think that you may have a better idea or solution to a problem or situation than your leader. But while this is a natural step of growth and one to be expected, by both the follower and the leader, it brings with it a certain dilemma.

*I experienced a situation in which I believed my perception of what was happening was more accurate than my leader. I was in a quandary, because I knew my leader knew what we should do, but I just thought my perception and idea would yield a better long term result. It was tough to step up and say my piece. But I did, and I learned from it, and so did my leader. She demonstrated leadership qualities I needed to learn.*

Probably the toughest step anyone takes is to step up and say something is not right as it relates to potential disagreement with leadership. It is scary to place yourself in a position where you are basically stating a position or opinion that differs from that of the leader who has been your coach, expert resource and support for your development process. However, followership demands you do exactly that, as the situation dictates.

Followership is built upon a base of personal character. If you see something taking place or have knowledge of a decision to be made that in your opinion is the wrong thing to do and you do nothing, wherein lies your character? However, you say, stepping up and saying what you believe needs to be said at the appropriate time appear to be contrary to good career management.

That takes courage. In my case, I had a positive experience and felt the power that comes with taking this step in the company of a leader that welcomed thoughtful opinion.

Leaders must encourage and respect opinions that differ from their own. If the leader penalizes dissent, the organization will fail because the best and brightest will see the writing on the wall and will keep quiet as they look for other jobs.

Followers must understand that leaders need to hear different perspectives. How else can a leader make a good decision, if all they see or hear is information that only supports their perspective?

*During the planning of a major exercise, a situation developed that ran exactly counter to my experience above. I remember sitting in the briefing room with the general and the staff as he was briefed about the planning process. When the general would ask if something had been accomplished, the colonels would invariably get up and say yes. I always found it so interesting, that as soon as the general left the room, the colonels would be like a swarm of bees together trying to figure out how they were going to do what they said they had already done. Why would they do this?*

*I found out during an exercise. The general could not pick up a phone at his desk and talk with the lead aircraft of the exercise strike formation that was thousands of miles away. Because of this, he literally yelled at and treated a colonel, who was a very hard working professional and excellent leader, for failing to do something the general wanted. He held him personally responsible and threw him out of the room (it was not possible for this situation to have been the colonel's fault–it failed through failure at the far end of the communication process). It was mean spirited and accomplished nothing other than generate negativity for the entire staff. No wonder no one ever wanted to say no to this general. He was not a leader through earned respect; he was a leader by position only. In this case, the leader failed the team. It would be difficult beyond reason for anyone to provide negative feedback to someone like that.*

This is a critical test of character for leaders and followers. Leaders who only ask for or accept information they want to get make poor decisions, because they do not have all the facts. In this case, they do not have the courage to accept that other positions or ideas may be as valid as or more valid than their own.

Followers who only tell their leaders what they think the leader wants to hear provide a disservice to the leaders decision making process and are equally responsible for the poor decisions that will follow. In both of these cases, neither party demonstrates the personal character necessary to support the roles they play.

Keep in mind, that constant criticism or nay-saying is not what courage is about. If someone has a bad attitude and disagrees for the sake of disagreement, then they will not last long.

This particular type of courage is about well thought out ideas and thoughts that interpret information from a different perspective than the leader. The leader needs to hear this perspective. This type of courage makes the team stronger and better. The courage to raise a different and potentially negative viewpoint than the leadership is something that leaders must encourage from their followers.

• <u>Self-Employment and Energy</u>

Courage is a self-generating energy source. This self-generation is purely based on energy. Where does that energy come from? Primarily, from the energy associated with self-employment.

Self-employment implies that you are on your own, dependent on your own energy, decisions and activity. It implies that the result of your choices determine your level of success or failure. For the purpose of our discussion we are not looking at this from a truly "self-employed" perspective, but an identification of the attitude of self-employment. The attitude of self-employment means you embrace the energy that only comes from reliance on your own capability, part of which is that tension or apprehension of potential failure.

Self-reliance is important, even within a team. As a leader, you have learned to rely on your instinct, analysis and business sense. You have demonstrated your abilities time after time, until you have come to believe you are the best judge of the moment.

As a follower you are expected to participate with others, bounce ideas off them and effectively manage all the other items we will discuss. However, you have not yet developed internal strength and confidence in your abilities. Once you begin to experience confidence in your abilities, this self-reliant attitude, while not arrogant, is self-employed energy. It is this energy that is critical for nurturing and development.

Leaders need individuals who clearly demonstrate self-employment through finding value in their own performance. Self-employed followers can be depended upon to ask themselves and their team tough questions, seek effective resolution and improve performance. Leaders need to know their followers are self-employed so they do not have to spend so much valuable time following up on performance.

Followership demands self-employment. It is critical to take responsibility for your own actions and your own growth. It is critical to demonstrate your self-employment by being there when the job requires it, not just during the hours of operation. Self-employment is vital for demonstrating another key building block—ownership.

Ownership is the ultimate stepping-stone to leadership, therefore leaders encourage and expect to see followers progress through to ownership. As self-employment demonstrates ownership, a follower must actively demonstrate this behavior.

Self-employed followers are the ones who take on the role of thoughtful dissenters. A thoughtful dissenter is not someone who disagrees with everything the company or the leader is trying to do. A thoughtful dissenter is not negative or working at cross purposes from the team. A thoughtful dissenter is simply someone who provides the leader with a candid evaluation of proposed directions based on their own knowledge and experience.

However, before you can be a thoughtful dissenter and respected as such, you must build credibility. Credibility, tied closely with believability, derives from all the items we discuss throughout this book, but especially in Chapter 4, Personal Characteristics.

Thoughtful dissent is not something you should exercise regularly. If you are on board with the basic direction of the leadership team and direction of the organization, it really should not be a regular practice, nor should you be looking for things to dissent about. However, there are times when your perspective gives you a unique view of how a decision or direction might play out that the leader might not see. In this case, failure to provide that thoughtful dissent is a failure of followership.

Followership demands you provide insight to your leader when you have it. If you perceive that a client may be moving to pull their business unless certain changes occur and you do not provide this intuitive insight to the leader, you are not providing effective followership. If you think that a certain decision will affect business in a way that is contrary to the leaders stated intentions and you do not inform the leader, you are not providing effective followership.

Leaders must have followers who will provide them candid feedback on decisions and direction. Otherwise, the leader might make a serious mistake without knowing it, with a negative impact to the business. This feedback is critical for ensuring all aspects of decisions are considered, and is a critical need for leaders.

This feedback comes from the self-employed energy of the follower, which is energy that comes from the courage to think, to inform and to act. Courage then is the basic energy generator for followership.

- Bias

Human relations are the linchpin of effectiveness when leading. Without a solid understanding of people, you cannot lead effectively. One of the issues within human relations is how we treat others, and more specifically, our bias towards others. In this regard, it is critical to be non-biased.

Being non-biased is hard, simply because it takes you outside of yourself and forces you to see things in a separate light. Being non-biased can be hard, simply because you will have to make decisions and express attitudes that may be contrary to those of your friends and place you in a position that isolates you from biased positions.

Most people transition into a supervisory role after having been associated with other workers. As a co-worker with others, we often share similarities with them, simply because we "go along to get along" and am attracted to like people to associate with. Everyone does not go through this phase, but it is a general norm that affects most people. In any event, once someone is promoted to supervisor, there is a necessary transition away from the commonality with the former co-workers and toward a commonality with other supervisors and leaders.

The transition itself is partially difficult because the biases shared with previous co-workers must be broken. Biases such as anti-supervisor, believing the company is out to get everyone, not liking people just because, not liking minorities or supporting equal treatment; in short, there can be a lot of biases shared privately with co-workers when none of them are actually responsible for anything.

But suddenly you decide to seek a promotion and get it. Now what? You cannot operate using the biases you shared previously. You are now responsible for equal treatment and fairness in the workplace. Your former co-workers may or may not like the fact that you are now different than before, or that you know how they truly feel about certain things. However, to be truly effective and progress, you must be non-biased. You must be the honest broker. You must ensure everyone you have responsibility for feels they are being treated fairly by treating them fairly.

In this mode you create the sense of your character. The tough decisions we must make to be the person we must be are stressful. Stress and growth define and build our character.

I have seen numerous individuals fail in this transition. They simply could not stop being one of the guys. They made decisions that were based on previous bias and ultimately (and quickly) failed. Failing at the very bottom of the ladder of followership clearly informs people that someone is not cut out to be a leader.

*I recall one individual who was a very good performer. His sales and customer service were excellent. He often volunteered to participate in activities other than the standard work. He gave all appearances of someone seeking a step up.*

*During the interview process, he provided the right answers to the questions, gave good examples; in short, he did it right. He appeared to be very happy he received the promotion.*

*Almost from the first day, however, he did not separate himself from his buddies. He went to the smoking area with them, he went to lunch with them, and took breaks with them. He appeared sulky in meetings and always brought up negative perspectives on processes or ideas.*

*Finally, he made a couple of decisions he should not have made in regards to employees on his team. He made the decisions based on his and his buddy's biases towards certain individuals. Once he did this, he was coached and disciplined. However, even with constant feedback on the cause for his action and the need to separate himself from his previous associations, he could not—or would not. Very quickly his employment decision was supported and he was allowed to pursue his success elsewhere.*

This step, this act, of changing your behavior to fit the needs of the team, takes courage. Without courage you experience an internal fear that defeats your goals. Poor self-esteem supports failure. Lack of courage cements it. It was a lack of courage that caused this young team leader to fail. It was not skill or ability to do the job. It was the courage to do it right.

- Counseling And Discipline

It takes courage to step up and counsel individuals on behaviors and performance. Initially, it is just terrifying to be in a situation where you know they will be stressed. This increases your stress and can create a situation where both the counselor and the counselee are stressed.

Counseling is confrontation. Not conflict, but confrontation. As we confront small performance or behavior issues, we take the energy out of the big picture. Not counseling about small things, but waiting until they are big is when you may end up with conflict. It also would mean you did a disservice to the counselee.

Confronting someone about poor performance can be difficult. However, when leaders effectively coach and support new supervisors, they teach them the skills they need to successfully coach. Even so, counseling requires courage.

The person you are counseling does not know what is coming. Not knowing creates a sense of fear. You, as the counselor, must have courage for the person you are counseling. You must be strong for both of you to provide the energy to successfully complete the counseling task. You must control the session and achieve a vision of success that both of you can share.

There are many books and guides on effective counseling. The simplest advice I can give you to be successful is to be present when you have a counseling session. You want to apply good body language in your seating arrangements. You want to be sure to raise your empathy to a high level. You want to ensure the counselee fully participates.

I have seen timid people go into a counseling session as counselors. I have usually seen them experience limited success, simply because without the courage to be confident in the face of an unknown response, they have not been able to withstand the stress of counseling and have allowed themselves to fail. This in turn fails the person who needs the support.

Counseling takes strength, confidence and courage. Confronting takes courage. A more intense format for confrontation is discipline.

Discipline is taking a step beyond conversation about performance and attempting to modify the behaviors that generated the performance through defined steps to force change. Discipline can be hard and very uncomfortable. Disciplining people also takes strength, confidence and courage.

When you reach the point in time that discipline is required, you are either recognizing a single significantly negative behavior, or you are providing closure to a series of negative performance behaviors. In both cases, the key is that you are addressing a person's negative behavior, or else you would not be stepping into discipline.

It is easy to tell someone they are screwing it up. It is easy to point at them and place blame on them and make them feel incompetent. It does not take courage to do that. Instead, it takes callousness or arrogance.

But that is not what a discipline session is for. Discipline is designed to modify behavior through the application of force. The only way you will ever modify someone's behavior (and not all the time) is to dig. Digging requires empathy, patience and a non-judgmental attitude. That is hard and takes courage.

In addition, discipline takes the ability to remain open-minded and look for opportunities to capitalize on things the disciplined individual says. If you are callous or arrogant, you will not be focused on finding these queues and will miss these opportunities.

I have seen many discipline sessions go wrong because the person doing the discipline was nervous, scared, or callous. The courage of discipline is that you must open yourself up in order to truly empathize with the individual, and if you do not empathize with them you may not find the key to unlock the person's potential.

Discipline is the last step in behavior modification. However, it is a necessary step to show all employees that they are important, and that you will work hard at trying to help them be successful. Just firing someone because they screw up, or not taking any time to work with someone who is not performing well but allowing them to fail; these are not steps in discipline.

Leadership demands effective and competent employees. Followership demands expertise, knowledge and experience with changing people's behavior in order to get the best from them and support the business of the organization.

Followership, therefore, demands a certain level of courageousness. Followership demands you take action when the level of your conviction is so great that to do otherwise would be a disservice to your self, your employees and your leader.

Listening to your conscience tells you when you have been courageous or not. Listen to the little voice within. It usually steers you in the right direction.

Followership demands empathy and understanding with employees to remove obstacles and change their behavior, as needed, to benefit the team. This takes personal courage to ensure success.

It takes personal courage to face your fear and decide to commit yourself to the highest values in followership. It takes even more courage to accept these as your own personal characteristics and move forward into ownership.

Courage is an intrinsically vital quality each of us must possess in order to choose to improve our lives. Without courage, you will not stand up for your rights when you are being abused. Without courage, you will not stand up to the playground bully. Without courage, you will not make the effort to rise above the expectations of your economic reality. Without courage, you will not effectively improve your self. Courage is the first stop for all of us.

## Followership Application:

Fear, as they say, is the mind killer. Fear can keep you from acting or speaking. Fear can knot your throat and stifle your performance. Fear is something we all experience and must learn to deal with. Fear is, at its very foundation, a primal human emotion. As humans, we have learned that failure to act in the face of fear is self destructive. It is called cowardice and brings no good result. These thoughts only increase the energy in the fear itself.

Because of this overriding emotion called fear, we have a word to describe what taking action in the face of fear is. This word describes something that is high up in our list of actions we deem as valuable and honorable. That word is courage. Courage is a personal demonstration of overcoming fear. Someone who demonstrates courage receives our highest praise and respect.

In the career progression described in this book, courage is placed in the same high esteem as any other value. Without courage you will not stand up and tell your leader information or perspectives that are different from what they want to hear. Without courage you will provide only lip service to your employee's needs, but not the deep empathetic support they may require. This becomes critical as a measurement of your confidence and ability.

Standing up to speak a different tune is not being rude, disrespectful, arrogant or mean. Contrarily, as you have been developing personal character traits you have been continuously supporting the growth of respect, patience and honesty. As you have been developing your communication skill you have been continuously practicing personal communication and have established a very good relationship with your leader.

Likewise, in the role of counselor and disciplinarian, your role is to both learn how to truly be effective and provide the support your leader needs to maintain an efficient and productive workforce. Providing the counseling, coaching and discipline necessary to achieve this takes considerable personal courage.

At this stage you continue these activities, but instead of remaining the constant pupil, you shift into the role, ever so gently, of equal. Not superior, as that would be a demonstration of arrogance and would violate everything you have been learning and demonstrating in your development process, but equal.

The goal is to earn respect through actions you take. This enables you to discuss situations in such a manner that you can disagree with your leader in such a way as to support the continuance of the relationship, but with the growing understanding that you are independent and capable of seeing things in a different light.

**Leadership Application:**

With all the fear your followers must work through, it rests on your shoulders to alleviate their fear of speaking up. With all the fears your followers must work through, it rests on your shoulders to help, coach and teach them how to effectively coach, counsel and discipline individuals on their team. Without your support of their voice, they will not learn how to use their voice and will remain silent.

Leadership demands that you speak about courage and even give examples when you were courageous. You must ask them to analyze information and see what they learn from it and recommend before you give your interpretation. You must encourage and support their ability to speak.

Leadership demands that you conduct counseling and discipline sessions with your follower in attendance, and participate in their sessions. Leadership further demands that you discuss objectively what you observed and provide the very same coaching style to your followers that they need to emulate with their followers.

Followers are transitioning through life. They are learning not only how to do their job, but accepting responsibility for others as they begin to take on more accountability. There are implications to employment. As many followers are in their younger employment years, they quite often have young families. This adds even more fear when it comes to disagreeing with the boss. As they are also similar in age and circumstance to their employees, being an effective coach or disciplinarian takes even more courage and skill.

This also adds even more responsibility to you as the leader to provide an environment where they can spread their wings, so to speak, and open their mouth to speak what they see, even if it differs from what you see. As a leader, you need this for a couple of reasons.

First, you need this so you can truly understand how they analyze, interpret and visualize performance data in order for you to both coach effectively and better understand what they mean when they say what they say.

Second, you need this because you cannot afford to become an island unto yourself and only have people who tell you what you want to hear. This is the path to failure.

I remember situations in my career where people only told the boss what they believed he wanted to hear. It was never a pretty sight.

We often question whether people at the top of organizations truly know what is happening down below. It is a truth that the messenger is often shot. It is no wander that people are afraid to speak out loud in situations where they fundamentally disagree with the leader's perspective.

Again, I must reiterate this—it is absolutely critical for you, the leader, to appreciate the divergence of voice in your team. It is not that you want everyone to look for reasons to disagree with you and create chaos. Rather, it is that you need to hear that lone dissenting voice that just may have it right out of a crowd of "yes" men.

In this, it takes courage from you, the leader, to accept the thoughtful dissenter as a true team participant.

# 2

## *Building the Foundation*

I would like to take a step back so we can move forward. Too many times, we do not apply life's lessons in our day to day activities. Instead, we often use data and statistics in our decisions (which is not bad, but is not the "whole person" we are evaluating.)

People are much more complex than the numbers make them appear. And critically, the development process is not a numbers event. The metrics we use to measure performance are created based on results we get *after* we have developed them as a measure of their ability to apply the skills we have taught them and primarily as a tool to identify additional skill or knowledge development they may need.

The lessons we learn and use for development are a culmination of all the lessons we have learned over time. These lessons are then applied daily to individuals who are each very unique and very similar to the other individuals around them—but all of them are at different developmental locations. How do we develop leadership in such a chaotic environment?

The process of growing leadership does not simply begin with a promotion to a supervisory or leadership position. Nor does it begin with the first entry level job. Rather, the individual's journey to leadership begins at birth.

All experience lends itself to development of the personality that is the person who enters the work force and gets promoted to a leadership position. Understanding not only your own development but the development and timeline position of others will greatly enhance your ability to perform as a leader, and help you understand that the development process continues through life—it doesn't simply end when you get the job. For that reason, this chapter begins at the beginning and works through towards acquired leadership behavior.

- Complexity and Variance of Development

Life is complex. It is far too complicated to separate work behavior from personal behavior. Our behavior crosses lines. How we do what we do does not stop just because we are at work, or because we get a promotion. All the things we do, all the behaviors we are, become our experience, which is again, who we are. Our experience then shapes our development and is in-turn developed by our behaviors and choices.

Because of the nature of these relationships and how interwoven they are, it is important to understand where they come from. We need to think about and take a look at how our attitudes and behavior traits either help or hurt us. Understanding these personal behaviors will help us reduce the impact of bad traits in our life and help us increase the impact of our good behaviors.

I find it interesting to watch people. I often find myself asking myself questions about the person I am watching. I ask things like, "Where did that behavior originate?", or "I wonder how that behavior helps her be successful?" Asking myself questions helps me focus on the behavior itself and how it supports or detracts from the overall performance of the person I am watching.

Taking a long look at life and how we develop also provides insight. How are you supposed to understand the best way to coach, discipline or enhance someone's performance if you don't understand why they have certain behaviors? When you take it a step further, you realize that it is important to understand where someone is on their life and personal behavior development timeline.

*Note: This is one of the drivers to effective coaching—understanding what motivates someone. This takes personal time and attention to discover what makes someone tick. It brings out their background. Talking about someone's past and experiences is a great tool for building empathy—more on that later.*

One of the reasons for this is quite simple. People have different behaviors and needs at different times in their life. A young single person entering the workforce has far different needs than an older, more experienced worker with kids. Coaching them, disciplining them and helping them improve takes different steps. How effective you are at working with both of these different individuals depends on how well you understand them and their needs. Otherwise, you are putting "band-aids" on things that need surgery; or worse yet, operating on things that might only need an aspirin.

*A young lady worked for me who simply did not seem to be able to get the job done. I asked her supervisor to tell me about her. The supervisor did not really have a lot to say about her, just that she was really being a problem by not doing the job in a good quality manner. No offense to the supervisor concerned; but that did not tell me a thing I needed to know in order to provide a recommendation for her improvement.*

*I asked the young lady to stop in my office. When she did, I moved around from my desk and we sat facing each other, with no barriers between us. I asked her some questions about the job and basically showed an interest in her as a person. She soon opened up and began talking. It turned out she did not know she was performing badly. She was used to being put down at home no matter what she did, so she just assumed work was the same.*

This is a case where the person is living the experiences and behaviors of their life and do not know anything different. Obviously, the behavior of poor performance is unacceptable, but so is the lack of knowledge in not understanding that good performance is rewarded. The first one is a workplace practice, but the second is a learned life behavior.

In order for the individual to become a strong team worker, this behavior must be understood and addressed. After talking with her, I talked with her supervisor. I coached the supervisor on the need to learn observation and team development, as well as specific ways to coach this young lady to success. After discovering one aspect of her expectations, we modified, over time, her performance through active discussion and constant reminders. She later became a very good team supervisor.

Another thing to keep in mind is about you. Where are you on your lifeline? What expectations or needs do you have that color your behaviors and performance? Do you allow your expectations to cloud your ability to effectively see what your team truly needs? It is important to be aware of how you relate to everyone else. You must, in the old saying, know yourself.

- Relationships & Fellowship

This chapter discusses these types of issues as an overview to establish a foundation for the central theme of leadership growth found in the remaining chapters.

As humans, what is the first thing we do? The first thing we do as humans is establish relationships. This process never changes. Birth itself is the beginning of the cycle of our knowledge. We all experience it. Most of us then establish the first and most important bond we will experience in this life, and the one that will influence us more than any other. We establish a personal relationship with our birth mother and father. Not everyone has this luxury, and not all experiences are positive. But generally speaking, this is the main event.

This initial relationship, or lack thereof, has implications and ramifications for the life of the person concerned. By the way, for purposes of this discussion, we will assume the paradigm of having a positive experience with both birth parents during this phase.

Why start a book about leadership with birth? In order to provide effective leadership, coaching and motivation for the humans in the organization, it is necessary to understand the human condition. It is important to have a perspective of the human condition that is as all encompassing as possible. As we discuss coaching and counseling later on, having a good understanding of human life cycle knowledge will become apparent. While this is not a psychology lesson, it would be a wise decision for anyone desiring a position of leadership to take some basic psychology classes.

I have heard some say that operating at this level of understanding of the human condition is not necessarily a good business practice. Some say that people should be treated as a part of the business process only, and not as individual people. I truly and deeply disagree with this. If you want people to commit their energy and effort toward success, you must treat them with respect and decency. Anything less is creating a self-fulfilling prophecy of poor expectation, followed by poor performance as people live up to your low expectations, and ultimate failure. People need to feel needed.

The expectation and pattern we establish in human relationships begins during this first few years. How people respond to us, our self esteem, level of interest shown, ability or desire to control, our communication ability, hand/eye coordination; all of these and more begin at this age.

*A **Side Note**, it is incredibly important for parents to pro-actively develop their children. After all, you are developing a human you hope will become a mature, competent adult; not raising an entertainment toy. These first few formative years have the most significant impact on the life of every person.*

*Psychiatrists and psychologists spend considerable time digging back as close to these foundational experiences as possible in their attempt to help someone correct or overcome an emotional situation in later life created during this time. Early childhood development is critical for the establishment of behaviors that will be reflected in performance throughout someone's life.*

This is the beginning establishment of fellowship. Fellowship is the need to establish relationships with our fellow human beings and with our spiritual self. Fellowship begins before birth and continues through death. We never tire of needing relationships. After all, relationships define us. Relationships create us. Who we are interacting with people is who we are.

*A Side Note: Who we are interacting internally with God defines our character. As human beings we have a split down our middle that has human, physical life on one side and spiritual existence on the other. God lives in our spiritual existence. Finding the path to bring God into our life to fully mesh the reality of physical existence with our spiritual existence provides a whole person approach to life. This struggle or situation continuously impacts our ability to apply all lessons learned in all aspects of our life.*

Today more than ever, organizations must find ways to support spiritual existence as well as physical existence. Providing the basics, like a paycheck and safe environment, are necessary for basic safety and security needs. However, when you need your employees to perform at a higher level you must do more. Providing quiet rooms for time out enables people to get away for a few moments to reflect and think. Sponsoring or subsidizing membership in health clubs for employees to exercise and improve health away from work supports both the physical and spiritual performance. Physical and spiritual performance is critical in that they provide a platform from which the person performs and assists in establishing the culture and environment of the organization.

I have seen this phenomenon in several organizations. When the leadership provides encouragement and support for the whole person of the team, the team responds. When the leadership is only concerned about the financial return they can get before they do anything, the denial of encouragement also causes the team to respond. It does not take much to encourage people. But it does take time, energy and effort. This is a small price to pay for the improved attitudes and response you get. It all comes down to how we relate to others.

• Developed Behavior Impact

The way we learn to relate with people is a critical skill in life. Did you cry until you got your way as a baby? Did you whine and get your way as a pre-teen or teen? Chances are that in later life you will still be tempted to whine to get your way. Ask yourself a few questions about this behavior. Is that a pattern of behavior you appreciate or respect in others? Does that behavior type exemplify leadership? Do leaders whine? Better yet, can someone truly rise up to be a leader if whining to get their way is the skill they utilize? I assume you agree the answer to all of these questions is no.

Whining is not an adult way to communicate or negotiate. Whining is a direct reflection of the child behavior of crying and appeasement by parents. Business demands adult behavior, not parent-child behavior.

I have seen this demonstrated countless times. Kids leave home and get their first real job and they bring their worst behaviors with them. This is one reason I believe it is important to talk about professional work behavior. A lot of new employees have never really been exposed to this and will continue to behave as they would at home to get their way with mom or dad. To say this is poor business behavior is an understatement! But it is not that they are bad. It is just that they need knowledge and coaching. Knowing what to look for gives you the edge on being effective in addressing their behavior.

Also, as parents, we have an obligation to ensure we do not teach our children to cry or whine to get their way. We need to be aware of this behavior and the ramifications it will have in later adult life. As parent's, we must recognize that the singular purpose of raising a child is to produce a competent adult. Children are not entertainment. Their behavior as a child will be their behavior as an adult. As such, appeasing your child does not an effective adult produce.

Knowing why someone whines is a helpful tool in effective coaching and counseling. People who demonstrate this behavior do so because it is who they are and they have gotten to where they are using this tool. This behavior must be addressed in a supportive manner. However, it must be addressed in order for the individual to have the opportunity to modify their behavior and eliminate this negative behavior characteristic.

Think about the behaviors you see in the workplace. Ask yourself why some people come to work late and why some arrive on time. Perhaps people who are late did not learn to respect others, but did learn that tardiness is acceptable. This is probably because in their childhood tardiness was tolerated. However, people who are on time learned to respect others and learned that tardiness was not tolerated. This is, in almost all cases, a learned behavior.

Traits of character, which we will discuss throughout this book, develop in these formative years. While the foundation for the strength or weakness of these character traits are established through example in these years, more reinforcement and development occurs later.

We learn to communicate in this earliest phase of life. We learn body language and speech. We learn our value through interaction with others. We learn how to understand the world around us as we learn the names of the things around us. We learn our place in the world as we learn the family relationships we are part of, and then expand to friends, teachers and others in life.

We learn how to get what we want through communication. Remembering the whining comment above, it is important to remember that most of the things we learn about anything at this phase of life we learn through the auspices of our parents. Effective parents will consciously provide the support we need without reinforcing negative behaviors. It is much easier to think as a parent when your child has learned that whining, crying or yelling do not get rewards. This reduces the amount of time your children spend in these states and provides you more time to be able to think clearly about what to do to support your child's development.

For these reasons, it is also important to think about your work force. How many of them did not have effective parents as role models? As a society we do not fully provide future parents with the knowledge or training to effectively parent. The children we bring into the world continue this into their adult life.

*A **Side Note:** While there is no way, as a supervisor or manager, to truly determine what type of parenting your employees experienced, you can draw some conclusions based on general observation of performance and behavior. Just remember that without actual knowledge of someone's experience your observations are only one part of the puzzle. Because of that, never use your general observations about someone to cause you to make a determination about them—get the facts about actual behavior and performance first.*

The positive aspect of this is that we can change our behavior to establish the behaviors we need for success, but only if we have mentors and coaches who work effectively with us to enable us to experience a positive change process. This is fundamentally why I believe leadership behavior can be taught—if the process and approach are positive and well managed. That is one premise for this book. While you read about these personality characteristics, evaluate yourself and the organization members on your team.

Communication is one item we like to believe separates us from the animals. However, even animals communicate. We believe that we communicate on a higher level. However, more to the truth, we communicate about our emotions and feelings. This is the clear distinction between the animals and us. We know we exist; we feel it, talk about it, work on it and make decisions because of it. Leadership is about emotional expectation management as well as any other thing. It is the touching of these emotions that define the leader. It is finding how to motivate people in a positive synergistic manner that defines great leadership.

Behavior I have observed many times are judgments made about people because of how they feel. This is improper and wrong behavior. It is never wrong to feel. Ever. It is the decisions or behaviors made based on feelings that can be evaluated or discussed. However, never criticize someone for having feelings. Feelings are real to the person having them. Feelings are who each of us truly are. To criticize someone for their feelings reduces the respect they have for you significantly, and alienates them from the group. Leadership demands respect for the feelings of others _and_ successful management of the behaviors associated with those feelings through effective communication.

If we do not learn to effectively communicate with others, we handicap ourselves for a lifetime. This early communication is the central developmental tool for our life. It is central to our overall adult behavior. We learn all we learn through the prism of communication. If the prism is faulty, we learn in a faulty manner. It is imperative then, that the parent work to create a legitimate prism for the child to see through.

- Impact Begins Early

Many parents are afraid to make what they believe to be harsh decisions for their children. For example, many parents allow their children to see horror movies. However, the images portrayed in these movies imprint an indelible image in the minds of these children that taints their prism for the rest of their life. Much more appropriate would be to keep these images away from the child and allow them to make the decision after they become an adult, as to whether or not to watch them. This is the position of parental responsibility.

Children who are allowed to have their way expect to get their way. In the "real world," it just doesn't work that way. This false expectation, that you always get your way, will set the young adult up for failure because they haven't learned the negotiation and compromise skills necessary to gain success.

In another respect, think about our society and the instant gratification culture we have become. Children who get what they want just because they want it create an internalized set of expectations that clash with reality in life.

Children who are exposed to everything at an early age have limited or tainted understanding of the sacredness of life or the sanctity of life. They have no purity

within to use as a foundation to create a life containing purity. This in turn negatively influences the spiritual growth of the person. I am not saying that any kid
who has seen a horror movie is damaged goods. I am saying any kid who has been
exposed to horror movies is different from one who has not been exposed.

What are the ramifications to the adult in these situations? It hinges on the
impact to the development of character.

- The development of character hinges on the establishment of value.

- Value comes through establishment of an enlightened understanding of place
  in life.

If a child perceives a horror movie as a reality-based event, it modifies the
child's set of values as the scenes of the horror movie show the deprivation of
value in the interactions of the participants of the movie. This has impact. The
impact of this is to the foundational values being created within the child. As
these values are changed or twisted, the adult will be changed as well.

It is not only in this form of communication that life is changed. Children
observe the news, they see movies of all ratings, they play video games, they see
television shows, they see commercials, they read headlines, they are online; in
short, kids are impacted and influenced in a multiplicity of ways at all times. The
cumulative impact of these observations is the issue. The modification to the
foundation of internal values is the direct impact.

The affect on the overall relationship building process of the child is very
important. These social relationships provide the foundation the young adult will
utilize in their daily performance and expectation management. If the relationship building process is less than stellar, the resultant relationships will be less
than stellar. This can lead to a person in the work environment who does not
know how to effectively work with others, cannot demonstrate effective team
building, cannot coach or understand the true process of assisting in the development of others.

- Social Relationship

These are all critical issues the leader must be able to effectively evaluate. You
must be able to read others to determine what their specific development needs
are and apply that coaching in such a way as to gain the improvement you seek
without negatively impacting their performance. It is not an easy task, but it is
very doable. This is the most important coaching skill for the leader to master.

Social relationships and the skills learned at this early age of personality development are very influential on the future performance and behavior of the individual. Everything is based on relationships. The entire spectrum of human development, existence and purpose centers on relational activities. Having underdeveloped social skills limits the individual from achieving higher levels of success.

As a leader, you must recognize that some individuals need socialization development. It is therefore critical for you to reach deep into an understanding of the processes involved in the development of social skills to see where you can best target your support for the individual you are working with.

Take a hard look at the behaviors demonstrated by the individual. What is it, specifically, that you perceive as less than where you believe it should be? Is the new supervisor unable to effectively provide performance based critiques or conversation with his or her subordinates? Why would this potentially develop in a person?

In a layman's eye this could be from a couple of things, such as a negative experience at a younger age in which some criticism was given that caused pain—either to the individual or to the other person involved—that had a tremendous impact on the individual you are working with. Without trying to be a psychologist, it would be helpful to have a conversation about the subject of providing feedback and asking the individual to provide some examples from their past of success and failures. Talk about the most negative experiences and how they happened; have a conversation about the proposition that they probably happened because either one of or both of the parties to the negative incident did not have any training on effective feedback. Work with the individual to establish clear processes and guidelines on giving feedback.

It may even be appropriate for you to sit in on a couple of sessions until the individual gains confidence in this new skill and can effectively provide feedback unsupervised. In this manner you can teach the skill set of providing feedback in a supportive manner and develop this confidence in your subordinate.

- Value

As a leader, it is imperative you be aware of the spiritual struggle inside each person. Some people you meet will be experiencing significant difficulties effectively balancing their life. The development of the balance between human and spirit involves the establishment of enlightened values. True leadership demands these values. People who are having a tough time with spirituality have a hard time demonstrating these values.

Values are developed early in life. Values are reinforced and empowered later in life, but if you get handed a set of poor values as a child, chances are you will keep those values as an adult. People can change; however, it is a very tough road.

If someone is demonstrating poor value development, it will be hard to turn this around. Questions of honesty, ethical behavior and trust are hard to overcome. Usually the proper response is to let people go who fail in these areas. It is critical for parents to set the right example for their kids to grow these values early and deeply in their kids. It is critical for leaders to model these behaviors in every day life.

These values, communication skills and other traits being developed through youth culminate in the establishment of effective interpersonal relationships. This is a key development stage. Usually this occurs in the teen years.

Effective interpersonal relationships are a preview of the ability to lead, manage, coach and support a group of people. These basic skills are learned in the early years and especially in the socialization years of adolescence in school. Interpersonal relationships teach us how to get along, manipulate or motivate others to achieve a desire of our own, get close to people and effectively communicate.

One of the first places where people get to demonstrate their interpersonal communication skill is their first job. Most people get their first job in a position that gives them some money to get through school, or a very entry level position after completing school. In either case, starting your first job is a very leveling experience. Everyone experiences it.

All the lessons of life learned up to this point, the values of work, work ethic, coordination ability, organization skill, communication; everything is tested in this new environment. This new employment environment provides the field to take these learned behaviors out to see how they match up with other people's behaviors and begin to perform in a larger, more meaningful environment.

Of specific interest for new employees and employers, is the ability demonstrated by the new employee to quickly master the basic technical aspects of the position. This is an obvious first step into the business world and it is a critical one. Leaders must evaluate the learning and application of knowledge ability of these new workers. The way in which frontline supervisors interact with new employees will greatly determine the future of these employees in the company and in the employment environment. Leaders must, therefore, understand the need for and provide effective oversight of these supervisors as they directly impact the new workers.

As new employees skills become satisfactory, they are able to demonstrate more than just the technical skills for the position. They begin to demonstrate an ability or inability to influence others. This is usually developed through the supervisor either asking for a volunteer to do an additional project, or each employee being selected to do an additional project. In either case, the working employee is evaluated to see what potential exists.

Demonstrating effective interpersonal communication skills may mean the individual demonstrates an ability to influence others. It may also mean the individual behaves in a way that naturally influences others, hence the "born leader" paradigm. In either case, once someone demonstrates the ability to influence others a change usually occurs.

This change is that the individual actualizes internally that they have a greater potential than performing just the work they are performing, because they understand they can effectively influence a larger group of people. When this occurs, the individual shifts into the final step before followership–demonstrating potential.

Demonstrating potential is a critical step. It occurs not only when the individual is desiring to move into a supervisory position, but at many times in life when you are working to clearly demonstrate you are performing at a level that demonstrates the potential to succeed in a higher or different position.

When an employee internalizes this idea and consciously works to demonstrate the potential necessary for a step up, it is a critical time for both the employee and the organization. Failing to work with the individual to provide challenges will cause the individual to experience a let down in emotional charge and potential loss to the organization. This is the perfect time to take this person's positive growth energy and move them into a new, more responsible position.

This chapter has covered a lot of ground. I want you to try to visualize the progression of the human from birth to the promotion to new supervisor/manager, and through the continuous development into leadership with higher and higher responsibility roles. Each person has unique experiences throughout their growth. Oftentimes we do not take the time to understand why people behave as they do. We sometimes wonder why a certain person who we think has potential does not "go for it." We wonder why someone behaves a certain way that appears anti-work focused and sets them up for failure.

Taking the time to honestly evaluate an individual's past, and working to truly empathize with them, enables the opportunity for influential change. Influential change is a basic necessity of leadership, and it begins with the relationships you have with each person you come into contact with.

## Followership Application:

As a newly promoted supervisor/manager, you are beginning your journey to effective leadership. This is not about processes or data management. This is not about getting reports completed on time or evaluating/analyzing data or processes. Leadership is about people. Everything else is management.

Management is a large part of the supervisor's job. Because you do have to review reports, analyze data; evaluate processes, performance and behavior. This is a critical skill in your growth process and one that must be taught alongside the leadership development process.

As a follower, discuss how you will be taught managerial tasks with your leader. Find out how the teaching process works and then embrace it fully. You must learn everything you can to be successful with your team and demonstrate your ability to progress through the development process.

Learning to be a leader requires you to work hard at selflessness. You must learn the traits of leadership and emulate them. You must carefully observe your internal motivations and feelings to ensure they are not causing you to behave in a manner that is received negatively by your team. You have a lot of work to do.

Taking the time to learn about people, how we are motivated, how we perceive our place in life, our expectations, fears and competencies, will provide you the information you need to mold a leadership style that can provide the leadership the team needs and be effective.

## Leadership Application:

As a leader, you must be able to understand the nature of not only your direct reports, but the entry level worker. You must understand their concerns, training, expectations, education, development and needs. Without this knowledge, you will be leading a management team but not leading the entire team. At that time you fail, because the working employees do almost all of the work, not the managers, and understanding their visualization of their place and expectations are critical to lead the whole team.

So we arrive now at the critical moment. You have decided to hire this working employee who appears to show potential and is competent in her work into a new management position. For both of you, this is the beginning of a new adventure. Hopefully, the experienced leader will bring all the skills necessary to the table to enable this new manager to fully succeed.

Take a look at Initial Assessment and Development in Chapter 14. This will further define what you should plan and consider as you begin the task at hand.

# 3

## *Communication*

The context of this book is that it is applicable to everyone.

- The new employee can utilize this book as a tool for self-development to begin preparation for future supervisory responsibility. Any book or process that discusses leadership cannot exclude the entry level employee. It is these individuals that leaders must lead for the organization to be effective. So we must take into consideration the skills, attitudes and expectations of these new hires.

- The new manager/supervisor can utilize this book as the followership process begins to ensure not only self-development, but ensure the leader provides a clear process and support for growth. These are the very people to directly associate with and influence the workers on the team. Without understanding their needs, skills and expectations, it is impossible to effectively lead them.

- The leader can utilize this book as the foundation for continued self-development, and for follower development as a mentor and coach of the new manager/supervisor.

- Lastly, the singularly most important impact of this book will be on personal development and choice. These cross all lines and are not limited to any particular organizational position or even a work environment. If there is anything I have learned it is simply that personal development and choice are what makes a person into a leader.

Most people actively change when they become a new supervisor. Basically this is because it is the first time they have been put in a situation where they were responsible for more than themselves. It is an eye opening experience!

I always enjoy promoting new supervisors. The look in their eyes is worth it all. The joy and fear that accommodates the promotion is almost tangible with them. I mean, this is it. For many, this is the experience they have dreamed of for a long time.

This is a very critical time for these individuals. This transition time is the most important for the individual and the organization. Effectively supporting the new supervisor through a process of development will provide the greatest impact to the most important individual–the working employee.

Implementing the process by which the most influential person, the front-line supervisor, can gain the most effect to influence the most important person, the working employee, is part of the primary goal of this process. This structure is critical to enable these individuals to attain the level of success their expectations provided them when they stepped up to the supervisory role.

For that reason, the leader should read this from the position of ensuring these steps are achieved in the growth/development process, and the follower should ensure they are working to achieve these goals as well as receiving the feedback and support necessary to improve their performance and career progression. As with all development processes—without the active engagement of both participants, the process fails.

- Communication

There are many skills the follower must master. However, there is one skill that has a direct impact on every other leadership skill. This skill is communication. For this reason the first major skill area we will discuss is communication.

What is communication? Communication is defined as the exchange of thoughts, messages, or information, as by speech, signals, writing, or behavior. This is a very good foundation for this discussion. However, for ease of use, remember that communication is the transfer of meaning. In all communication activities, meaning is transferred. The goal of effective communication is the transfer of your intended meaning.

How many times have you heard someone say something and heard it interpreted differently by others around you? Ever listen to someone talk and leave the room without a clear understanding of what was meant? That is failure to communicate.

Failure in effective communication is a leading reason for a failure in application of leadership skill. If you cannot communicate the vision, you cannot lead the team. If you cannot effectively speak or write, you cannot provide guidance, coaching, discipline or motivation to affect positive change. How then, do you communicate? How are you supposed to be effective?

*Important Note: In this book, I use the word "effective" quite a lot. The reason is that anyone can communicate, and we all do. This is not talking about pure communication, because we communicate all the time.*

*Just sitting and doing or saying nothing communicates a message. Your body language provides a message that others interpret. Communication is random, constant and ever happening. Every word you speak communicates. Everything you write communicates. Everything communicates. We all do it all the time. This is not what I am discussing.*

*What I am discussing is the very art of pro-actively communicating in such a way that you control your communication to achieve a purpose. Once you achieve that purpose, you are effective. Therefore, effective communication means communication that is pre-planned, pro-active or controlled in such a way as to achieve the purpose of the communication. Therefore, when I use the word "effective" in regards to any subject, I am implying a higher level of achievement than the basic process dictates.*

Communication includes a lot of parts to make the whole. To accomplish the goal of effective communication you must implement multiple processes and concepts. This is not about just talking. This is learning to and effectively communicating messages to others.

The need for this skill is simple. Life is about relationships. No other item has as much truth or weight as this simple statement. Leadership is about influencing people through your relationship with them; hence communication as a strategy for affecting relationships.

I have seen both good and bad communication. You know the communication is bad when it irritates, browbeats, denigrates, or is just hard to follow or quite simply does not make any sense. By the same token, you know the communication is good when you feel you have learned something, feel better about what you are doing, or feel included and understand the message.

- Empathy

There are a lot of parts and pieces to communication. But of all the areas we will discuss in effective communication, none has the weight of empathy. Empathy begins and supports the relationship building process. The results of empathy are greater commitment from individuals to the purpose and mission of the team.

Seriously, if there is no other lesson you learn in life, understand that the quality of the relationships you establish in life dictate the character you are perceived to have in life. Empathy is supportive of this because effective empathy enables you to establish a true relational contact with another person in an adult, non-judgmental manner.

Empathy is the art of placing yourself in someone else's shoes. Empathy is not sympathy, wherein you feel sorrow for the things that have happened to someone; rather, empathy is when you demonstrate both to yourself and the person involved that you fully understand their position.

This provides a substantial energy boost to both parties, as this empathy releases energy pent up through frustration in many people who fully believe that no one truly cares about them or understands them. Empathy shows you care enough to take the time to fully understand the person's perspective. This demonstrates your active valuing of another person. This establishes a true dynamic in growth of the relationship so established.

Leadership success hinges around your ability to influence others through the relationships you have with them. The key to establishing relationships is empathy.

Empathy means you are not a fake. Not being fake means you are there without distraction. Being with someone without distraction means you are working hard to empathize with them. You are not condemning them. You are not ignoring them. You are not belittling them. You are not judging them. Contrarily, you are actively working to understand how they see the world.

What is their perspective? What do they see when they look at the changes being discussed? Do they feel threatened? Are they confident? Are they ready to take on more? Are they at maximum capacity? Do they feel they are part of the solution?

There are hundreds of questions that should be going through your mind as you dig in and really try and understand someone's perspective. As you do this, you show the other person that you really care about them as a person; not that you sympathize with their feelings, regardless of them. However, you fully understand their perspective.

Empathy then, is the major gate-keeper to people's willingness to lower their barriers. If you are allowed beyond someone's barriers, you have truly established a relationship with them both you and they will feel. When they believe you actually do fully empathize with them, you have demonstrated great empathy and gained a person's respect and trust.

It is critical to gain people's respect as you move down the path toward leadership. Respect is not something you get because you show up. Contrarily, the failure of some workers beginning the transition into leadership is they expect or demand respect because of the position they hold. However, you earn true respect. You earn it through your demonstrated behaviors, such as your communication skill, which comes through learning to empathize with people.

It is critical to protect the empathic relationship. The trust you gain in this process is the link that keeps the relationship alive. If you haphazardly throw around personal details about someone that you gained through trust, you will destroy that trust. And you will never, ever be able to get it back. In this case you lose respect and the relationship. This is not to say you can never talk about someone's situation with an appropriate individual, such as human resources or your leader, as the situation dictates, but never throw around information haphazardly.

*I have seen this in action. I know a supervisor who talked about one of his employees to another employee. It did not take long before the word got to the original employee who was shocked and angry the trust had been broken.*

*When this employee charged into my office, I knew something was wrong, so I stopped what I was doing and took the time to listen. I discovered this employee had truly felt she had established a trusting relationship with her supervisor. Based on that, she had been honest about her impression of the work ethic of some other team members. Now she was angry that her comments had been spread around and the team knew she had spoken against some of them.*

*There truly was no way to salvage this situation. Try as I might, the employee felt too much stress in the work environment and eventually quit.*

The supervisor learned a very important lesson. You never, ever, talk about what an employee says to you to anyone other than your supervisor or human resources. You don't, because if you do you break the bond of trust that pulls people together into a relationship that supports performance.

You earn respect through your actions, such as maintaining trust. Your decisions reflect your integrity. The sum total of your performance, consistency and communication determines the respect you earn. Learning to be empathetic in your communication style will positively influence this process at the most important location, the individual personal level.

• Body Language

Following empathy, there is another overarching communication skill to master. The skill of understanding body language is critical. People say more with their bodies about their true attitude or feelings than with their words. Learn to read body language. Know what your own language is saying. Learn the type of language needed for specific situations.

*As an example, I worked in a location where the management staff had their office furniture set up so that when anyone came to the door, their back was to the door. What does that tell the person who comes to the door? It says that, "I am focused on things that are more important than you are; I am unapproachable; please leave me alone; and you are not valued."*

*How effective will the communication process be for the individual feeling they must breach this wall? In this case, communication was taking place, but not effective communication.*

In counseling situations, you must know what someone is saying with their body. Read the lowered eyes, the drooped shoulders, crossed arms and legs, whether they are sitting up and forward or back and slumped; all of these say something about the person. What are they saying? Are they saying with their words that they are excited to be on the team and will not be late again, but they are slumped, no eye contact and their voices are weak? How do you read that? It sounds like someone telling you what he or she thinks you want to hear, but with no confidence or truth behind it.

In this situation, you have to keep digging until you find what the true story is. Through this process, you establish empathy with the individual and get to the foundational issues affecting the person. From here you work together to build a new direction toward success. However, the point is, you have to know body language and what it means so you can identify when the body language of the person does and does not match their words.

On the other side of this coin is your own body language. Are you saying yes with your voice but no with your body? People can see through that approach. If you must relay bad news to someone, relay it with body and voice. Otherwise, you are perceived as an individual toying with people's feelings, may appear to be a manipulator or worse a bono fide controlling and arrogant smug individual. People can and do jump to conclusions about who you are based on what they see. This is the reason knowing what body language says and getting your own language in line with your words is so important.

It would be a good idea to read about body language to learn what people say with their bodies. There are some cultures that believe they should not look into the eyes of a supervisor, as it is a sign of disrespect. It is important for you to take the time to learn not only the generic body language of the present, but also any peculiarities of the workforce you hope to lead. Otherwise, you may insult, when you only want to support.

*A **Side Note:** As followers, it is imperative to take initiative to learn. As leaders, it is imperative to take the initiative to coach, support and set the example. Both have responsibilities for each follower's development; however, the ownership truly rests with the follower to learn personal knowledge, while working with the leader to develop fully the skill.*

• <u>Listening</u>

Another key technical ability that is necessary for building empathy is effective listening. Listening takes up more of our time than any other communication skill, yet we have the least exposure to learning how. It is not that we don't talk about listening; it is just that it is not a skill that is taught, except on rare occasions. Most of our communication skill development is spent being taught to read and speak. Yet we listen more than we write or speak.

It is odd that we do not take more time to teach effective listening. Many people confuse listening with hearing. They are far from each other, but intimately related. If you cannot hear, you cannot listen. However, you can hear without listening.

A major barrier to effective listening is quite simple: we love to talk. More than listening, people love to hear themselves speak, not necessarily in front of an audience, but love to speak nevertheless. Imagine a counseling session where the counselor does most of the speaking. Do you think she or he will learn anything about the individual's situation and actually help the individual concerned? I doubt it.

The essential ingredient in building empathy and effective coaching/counseling is listening. Listening requires more than just hearing the words. Listening is taking pro-active steps. These steps are applicable in many listening situations, not just in a counseling situation.

• Key to effective listening is preparing to listen. It takes effort and energy to listen effectively. It requires the ability to minimize distraction. It takes elevation of the importance of the person in front of you so you really focus to hear what the person is saying. Distractions come in many shapes and sizes, from too much noise, too hot or cold, no privacy, telephone calls, emails; many things are distractions. Being able to put all these distractions aside and truly focus on the speaker is a critical skill.

- Removing the distractions enables you to get to the true words of the speaker and attend. Attending is not just listening to the words they are saying, but also the concepts, concerns, fears, anxieties, joys and attitudes hidden underneath the words. Being able to gain a solid glimmer of the true person beneath the skin is critical to build the relationship.

- Neither of these steps matter, however, if you do not assign meaning to the speakers words. Attaching meaning gives you the ability to understand and learn. This gives purpose to the listening session, and in the case of a counseling session, enables you to respond appropriately.

An important tool in building empathy is clarifying or paraphrasing back to the individual you are working with. Convince them you know what they are saying, and you are effective with empathy.

In larger settings, being able to assign meaning and remember what is said is critical in learning the attitudes, directions and positions of the organizations leaders. What are they saying compared to what you heard beneath the words. This is the ground for discovering effective questions for clarifying.

I don't know how many times I have heard someone say something like, "I know he heard me, but I just don't think he got it." Meaning the person was not listening.

*A Side Note: Nothing is more irritating to me than to have someone keep working when I stop in for a visit. I have been on the receiving end of this several times in my career and every time the results were the same—the person who was too busy to focus on people failed.*

*One of the things I always tell my team is that when someone comes to you to talk, stop what you are doing and listen. Use common sense, so if it is necessary to schedule a time to listen because you are truly busy, schedule it. If you can only provide a few minutes, say so up front. But never, ever, keep working on the computer and pretend you are actually listening to the person talking. You are not effectively communicating with that person.*

In summary of listening, it is a separate skill you can and must develop. Effective listening means subjugation of your "self". Additionally, take advantage of the speed differential between speaking and thinking. Most people speak at an average of 150 words per minute, depending on the situation, such as personal conversation or speaking to a group. However, your mind can process at about 500 words per minute. This is a huge advantage.

The skilled listener will take advantage of this situation to listen for deeper meaning, relate the message to personal experiences, fit the message into a larger context or just learn. The un-skilled listener will allow the mind to wonder over imaginary events or daydream. Be skilled.

- Speaking

The speed differential is also critical in speaking. You can choose the pace of your conversation, depending on the situation at hand. With a higher processing speed internally, you can gauge the impact of the conversation on the other person or group and make corrections as necessary. Effective body language understanding is critical in this case. Interpreting body language is part of the items your mind is processing with the speed differential.

Of course, body language is impossible to read on the telephone or a conference call. Nevertheless, you can still tell mountains of data from voice inflection and tone. People will read the same from your voice. Take the time to think about the tone and quality of your voice on a call and make sure it matches your true attitude. Otherwise, change your attitude, if you are being negative unnecessarily.

Are you saying positive, motivational words; yet the team appears down and unenergetic? You may be missing something.

- What is truly the source of the teams rejected appearance?

- Are your words hitting where you need them?

- Should you shift to more of a question/answer format to get better input?

- Maybe you should modify slightly by discussing a different area and see what the response is.

The key is this—you can ask these types of questions in your mind while you are talking. You can respond to the needs of the person/team on the spot.

Speaking is not necessarily easy or fun. However, if you take the time to build it as a skill, you will be effective. Learning to enjoy it is a further step you develop as you move to ownership and leadership. Part of this process is to develop a keen sense of what the speaking is designed to accomplish. Think through the process to the goal. What do you want people to walk away from the communication knowing and feeling? How can you effectively target words to accomplish that goal?

Practice makes perfect. In the case of speaking, it is a very good idea to take some time to practice. Practice at home, in the office or anywhere else you have time. Then work hard at getting it right the first time, especially when you are communicating in your relational activities.

*I remember the very first time I had to give a speech. I knew my delivery would cause me to speak faster than normal. So I took the step to write on my note cards in capital letters: "SPEAK SLOWLY!" I knew that I would be nervous, but if I slowed down I would actually speak at a moderate rate. It worked and I did just fine. Since then, I always remember those written words in my mind when I speak. Otherwise, nervousness increases my tempo and affects my voice tone.*

*   Writing

The next area in our discussion is writing. Writing takes on many forms, from technical writing to emails to performance reviews. Learn to write effectively. This book is not about teaching you how to be an effective technical writer. This book is not about grammar or the specifics of writing, but is a quick review of each item placed into context for the overall development picture. However, you owe it to yourself to get the education you need in each area for success. Your employer owes you the help you need to get the knowledge and experience for proper development of these skills.

Writing takes a lot of work. Most people do not write the way they speak. There are rules of grammar that must be learned. There are rules for different types of writing. Learning the rules of the writing you undertake reflects dedication and commitment to high performance. Leaders need people who take the time to develop themselves and deliver excellent products.

The more you know about how to write, the more impact you can have on the organization. Many people cannot clearly transfer their thoughts onto paper in a cohesive manner. Learning this skill will propel you to higher levels of responsibility and inclusion. And remember, in writing, just as in speaking and all forms of communication, you must learn to effectively communicate, which entails transferring the meaning you intend.

Another aspect of communication is the appropriateness of the communication. Usually this is in reference to verbal communication, but it can transition into written as well, especially in email. You must take the time to understand several issues before you begin communication. You must understand the issues of who, what, where, when, why and how of the communication. Ask yourself some questions:

- Who should this be directed to?

- What is the most effective communication means?

- Where is the most effective place to conduct this communication?

- When is the most effective time to conduct this communication?

- Why is this communication necessary?

- How will this communication be received?

- What tone should I set?

- What do I intend or hope to achieve?

This is not all the questions, but it is a start. Essentially, you need to understand specifically why you need to communicate; the what, where, when, why and who of the communication; how it will be communicated; and last, but of utmost importance, how will this communication be received? How will the recipient react? What can I expect? What are my counter arguments, if necessary?

The point I am trying to make is simply this: before you go into any communication experience, think it through. Think about the needs, purpose, expected or desired outcome, people affected, corporate concerns, employee and financial ramifications and anything else you can consider that you believe is pertinent to this communication. This is not to prevent you from completing the communication. Rather, it is so you will be fully prepared and complete in the communication itself, plus prepared for follow-up questions and discussion.

One of the worst mistakes you can make is to send the "flaming spear" email. Let's say someone says something to you or you hear about something and it touches a nerve. You immediately react based on your feelings and type up an email or make a phone call that you have not thought through. What happens? You demonstrate that you are emotional to a fault, that you react but do not purposefully act, and that you behave in a less than adult manner.

These are perceptions you do not need. Remember that perception is reality. How you are perceived by people is the reality they operate under when thinking about you.

In the scenario above, it is always best to take time before communicating. For example, write the email and save it as a draft and come back to it the next day. Chances are you will discover your own words are inappropriate and will rephrase the email, if not cancel it all together.

Supervisors, managers and leaders usually complete some form of review on their employees. Effective communication is critical in this process; as otherwise, the employee will not have a complete visualization or understanding of how their performance is perceived and what steps are needed to improve that performance. If employees do not understand how to improve their performance, you are not driving performance or continuous improvement in your workforce. After you have completed a solid review, you will have ensured the communication is appropriate, and delivered in the correct manner.

Writing requires research, organization of thought, understanding of the topic, and awareness of the target audience. In reality, it resembles preparation for a speech, and is no simple task. Speaking requires a few other considerations as well. Researching the target audience takes on a whole new meaning when you will be face to face. Also, understand and know the location, as you need to be comfortable in your speaking. Again, you have to make sure everything is appropriate.

• Fairness

Appropriateness ties in with but is different from fairness. Appropriate communication is that which is geared to the communication process, rather than the perception of the process that relates to fairness. As an example, if an employee tells you privately that such and such are occurring, the appropriate thing to do would be to quietly address the issue as needed. The inappropriate thing to do would be to march out of the room with the employee in tow and publicly confront the person or situation.

There are many occasions where the level of communication intensity or type ties directly to appropriateness. You must always be aware that you are applying the specific level of communication necessary to address the need you perceive. Otherwise, your communication choice and style is inappropriate.

People need fair treatment because they want to be treated fairly. It is a simple thing, treating people with the humanity required to be fair. Most people are satisfied with this. If they believe you are fair, they will forgive much in content. However, if people perceive unfairness, the content of the interaction will be irrelevant.

This is extremely important. When you begin to conduct personal counseling and coaching, or discipline, you must be perceived as fair. Otherwise, everything you are trying to accomplish is for naught. Otherwise, the energy you expend and creativity you bring to the table is wasted.

Fairness is a very human trait. Fairness leads to believability, which is critical as you initiate or enhance relationships. Without believability, your efforts will be in vain.

Taking all of these threads of communication together and weaving a visualization of effective communication is the goal. Measure your effectiveness. Talk with your mentor and ask for a frank evaluation of your communication, with specific reference to your intended purpose and the actual delivery. Find out how you are perceived and work at improvement until you become very astute at delivering your intention.

Leaders need people who can effectively communicate the vision and message to the team. They also need people who can effectively communicate concerns and suggestions upward to be tools for the leader in other discussions with senior leadership. Being effective in communication, whether verbal or written, is a critical success skill. Nowhere else will your skill be more challenged than in coaching and counseling.

Coaching and counseling require an intangible ingredient called authenticity. Your entire communication process must pass the test and be judged authentic for the person you are working with to truly receive what you are attempting to impart.

Communication, as we have reiterated, is a two-way process. You do not effectively communicate until both parties have attended, attached meaning and learned. For this reason, you must realize you will be bearing the greater responsibility for the communication event, because you are aware of the process and working to manage the process to a successful conclusion. The person you are working with potentially has no training or knowledge of the fundamental communication process they are taking part in.

That is why it is critical you be authentic in your interaction. Because when you are, the other party will open up to receive from you, because they have judged you real. From this point, you have an honest moment to spend in providing support, motivation, or guidance and direction, depending on the interactions purpose.

This is a magnificent opportunity to touch another person's life. They will remember this moment in time, if you are authentic, because they will know they were valued. People do not forget the value we give them in our interaction. This is the underlying foundation of the purpose of effective communication—giving people a sense of value and worth through the process; and creating, enhancing and building valued relationships.

## Followership Application:

As we have discussed throughout this chapter, the need to learn effective communication skill is a primary skill development goal, in that most other skills evolve or rest upon your ability to effectively communicate. As part of your communication skill development as a follower, you must fully develop each skill and practice each skill until it is mature and effective.

Developing communication skill is not something you can fully accomplish on your own. As with anything else, to be truly effective you need good, productive feedback, so you can continue to hone your skills to maturity. There are many steps to take; however, the generalization of steps must, as a minimum, review the information outlined below.

1. Complete a communication self-assessment. For an example, see Chapter 14, Communication Assessment. This will help you identify your strengths and weaknesses in relation to the new position you have been hired or promoted to fill. All of us have strengths and weaknesses. However, the level of intensity of our strengths and weaknesses can vary depending on the position we are in. For example, you may hold a position as an analyst, and therefore have excellent writing skill–strength required. However, because you do not use your speaking skill, you may have below average speaking skill–weakness but not required. In your current position, the weakness does not hurt you, because it is not a required strength. However, if you are promoted or hired into a team leadership position, your speaking ability becomes a weakness that requires improvement to strength, while your writing strength remains a required strength. In addition, you may not receive the promotion you desire because your speaking skill is perceived as weak when it needs to be strong.

2. Request an evaluation of your communication skill by peers and leaders. These should be as encompassing as possible, considering not only the style of communication, but the appropriateness, intent, effectiveness, quality, voice tone, eye contact, and general body language in support of your communication, if verbal. Also have your written work appraised and evaluated for grammar, context and style.

3. Do not take feedback personally. Your leader/coach is giving you the information on what they see. Take this information and use it to complete your own self-assessment and work on improving the areas they mention as needing additional effort. Listen to the coaching they give and ensure you do not put any negative energy into it. If you believe you cannot improve and your level of belief pushes you to resent improvement efforts, it will not enable you to improve. This is, of course, assuming the leader/coach is providing unbiased, fair and valid feedback. If the feedback is not appropriate, this is an area for discussion with your leader/coach.

4. Read and discuss a book on body language. Some organizations provide reading libraries for employees and some do not. If yours does, borrow a book and work to understand it. If yours does not, talk with your leader about establishing a library and ensure a book or two about body language is included. Practice reading body language. Talk with your leader/coach about what you see in other people's body language to validate your perception. This is a way to calibrate between people, so the leader gains confidence in your perceptive ability.

5. Take on communication projects that involve various forms of communication. For example, seek an opportunity to present a briefing or address a group and ensure your leader/coach is present. Get feedback on your strengths and weaknesses so you can continuously improve. Be aggressive in finding opportunities to communicate. Always look to your leader/coach for feedback. We can always use good input to continuously improve our skill.

## Leadership Application:

As a leader, your skill and commitment to improving the skill of your followers will directly affect your effectiveness. Your followers will begin at different locations on the communication effectiveness scale. For that reason, one of the first tasks you have is to effectively assess their communication skill and identify areas that need urgent attention, some attention, reinforcement, or where they are very acceptable. Complete the Communications Assessment in Chapter 14 for your new follower.

After you complete this assessment, you must develop a plan to ensure your new follower has the opportunity, coaching and training necessary for effective communication. As you build this plan, keep in mind the specific requirements of the position they are entering, the preponderance of communication required, and the personality of the person being developed.

A follower who shows positive motivation signs and has a clear desire to improve their performance will be more accepting of your process. A follower who shows signs of believing they do not have a lot to learn in this area may not be as accepting. For both of these extremes and everyone else, it is important to develop these plans with the follower. Giving people the ability to participate in even their own performance development plan demonstrates fairness, ownership, and teamwork. All of these are ideas you want your followers to demonstrate and mimic.

Remember, it is not enough that you develop a plan. You are providing your followers with a role model. You are showing them how you want them to behave as you behave to develop them. As such, you, the leader, are always on display. Developing followers is not just a task; it is a revelation to them as to how they will eventually behave and how they will develop their followers.

Prepare and provide feedback to your followers as needed. Make sure the reception of the feedback is positive and well received. Otherwise, the feedback purpose can get skewed and the follower may become more agitated with the feedback than participative.

Lastly, remember that the leader carries the responsibility to ensure the entire development process is effective. It is a heavy burden, but one that will clearly have great rewards as your followers grow into excellent communicators and leaders.

# 4

## *Personal Characteristics*

In the previous chapter, we discussed communication. However, you will find that our discussion of communication is not isolated to a single chapter. Instead, everything in this book, and in fact everything in life, inevitably concerns or is interrelated with communication.

Effective communication, which is the goal, is grounded in establishing and living value based personal characteristics. The reason is simple: without these characteristics, you may communicate the letter of the message but be unable to deliver on the spirit or intent of the message; you may never be able to motivate others and a team, because you do not demonstrate the highest levels of character.

Character matters. Your character is your beacon that identifies safety when danger is all around. Without it, you would not know you were in troubled water and on the verge of disaster. Character is the sum total of who you are, doing what you do. Remember, it is not just important to know what to do, it is equally important to know how to do it and to do it in the right manner.

There are many characteristics we each must master to be truly effective leaders. There is honesty, integrity, adaptability, versatility, credibility, positive attitude, commitment, participation and believability. These are not all the characteristics of success. However, these are some I believe are essential to be an effective leader.

- Honesty

The first characteristic we will discuss is honesty. Why choose honesty first? Honesty is first because if you do not build a foundation of honesty with your self and with others, you will not be able to grow into leadership. Simply put, honesty is the first building block.

It may sound simple enough, being honest. However, I have seen many people struggle with this. Some people fail over ethical behavior, choosing one action over another because they were not truly honest with their self about their motivation. Let's look at an example in which a position comes open within the team.

*In this hypothetical example, the employees are competitors for this promotion. Let us say that you got the promotion because the performance under your responsibility was best. Let us further assume that you behaved in a way that did not fully support the other competitor's performance, even though your performance within the team had a direct impact on their performance.*

*Ask yourself some questions while looking in the mirror.*

*Did you want a competitor for a position to fail?*

*Did you truly work as hard as you could for everyone's success?*

*Is your personal success more important than the success of the team?*

*Be honest. Then ask yourself if your conduct was personally ethical. If you are truly honest, you cannot accept that you worked any less than the maximum of your potential. Otherwise, even your conscious thought that a fellow employee in the same organization failed is your guilty conscience speaking your inner truth.*

*In this type of case, everyone should have continued to work to their full capacity to ensure the success of the team and organization, and allow other factors to select one for promotion. Otherwise, the team loses anytime there is a promotion opportunity, because everyone has his or her own self-interest at heart. This might seem to be a normal idea, but it cannot be in regards to your honesty with your self. You must, at all times, perform to your full potential. Otherwise, you are not honest with your self, which will lead to your not being honest with others.*

How we communicate reveals our honesty. Here is another case where body language must match with verbiage or the vision crumbles because people see through you. Honesty is not always easy. If it were, it would not be a value, or a desired personal characteristic.

Honesty can be painful. Telling the boss your true opinion of actions or decisions is not easy. However, leaders need people to be honest. Without honesty, organizations fail. Honesty extends from your person throughout the organization, inclusive of shareholders. If the leadership had been truly honest, to the point of enforcing personal ethical behavior, neither Enron nor WorldCom would have happened. It was failed ethical leadership beginning with a basic lack of honesty that doomed these leadership teams.

Followership demands not that you follow the leader regardless of where they may take you, but that you weigh the decisions, provide honest feedback, and take responsibility for the decisions made. If you are in a situation where the decision made is, in your evaluation, dishonest, following through with that leader on that course is tantamount to complicity.

We know that the driver of the get away car in a bank robbery is guilty of robbing the bank just as surely as the person in the bank with the gun. Knowing the leadership is heading into a serious unethical choice and acquiescing is tantamount to complicity, which makes you as guilty of the unethical behavior as the leader. It is a tough situation.

Honesty demands respect. Honesty breeds wisdom, because a wise person understands the foundational position of honesty, and knows that internal honesty is required to learn in wisdom. That does not necessarily make it easy. The reward for maintaining an honest position in life is primarily that you see honesty when you look into the mirror. An honest person can see an honest person and gain a respect for self. A dishonest person can see the image of honesty through a veil of deception of self. A dishonest person can continue to lie to self and others and appear to be honest. However, this personality charade will fail in time.

- Integrity

Honesty builds behavior towards the establishment of integrity. Integrity is the glue that binds your words and actions into a single value. Integrity is both an act of conscious effort and a perceived value from others. The key is to behave in an ethical manner from personal choice AND be perceived as ethical by others.

This provides an internal/external integrity validation. Followership demands establishment of high ethical behavior. Else, the leader cannot depend on, believe in, or grow the follower into a leader. Leaders need ethical followers. Leaders need to know the words and actions, recommendations and ideas provided by followers are honest and ethical. If your behavior is such that your leader questions your integrity, you effectively end your career.

Remember, honesty with self tied to value based character development breeds integrity. This is the reason honesty is so crucial to establishing integrity, just as communication is so critical to effectively communicate honesty and integrity to the team.

Integrity demands toughness on self. As with so many of these issues, you have full ownership and control over the issue. You choose whether to be honest. You choose whether to be ethical. You choose whether to act with integrity. It is a simple choice, but with complex ramifications, not only for your self, but for others as well.

Failure to behave ethically, as I stated above, can result in careers end. Of further significance, however, is that behaving without integrity causes direct harm to other people. Integrity affects the environment of relational activity. Relational activity is a primary driver in leadership. Any behavior that negatively affects this activity negatively affects the organization.

*As an example, let us create a scenario. In this scenario, a very large computer system upgrade is imminent. Let us say the decision about which company to purchase this multi-million dollar software upgrade from is not, in and of itself, a question of integrity. However, the relational actions surrounding that decision could be integrity challenging.*

*For example, if the Chief Financial Officer recommends one selection and the Chief Information Officer recommends a different selection, the decision made will not be of an integrity issue, if the selection is on merits and cause. However, if it is later revealed the selection was made because one of the individuals offered favors, or favors were expected, or the company selected offered favors, etc., then the choice enters integrity's domain.*

*In this case, as soon as the favor is offered, the only choice to maintain integrity is immediate, full disclosure, and release of the individual complicit with the poor integrity direction or removal of the company offering the favors from the bid. Nothing else is acceptable. It is imperative to take action immediately upon knowledge in an ethical case. Anything other than immediate disclosure lends itself to implicit complicity with the poor ethical choice being made.*

It is a career ending action or a career building decision. Maintaining a close watch on your behavior, making the right decisions and holding your integrity high ensures you at least are equal on the playing field. From there it is your performance.

Ethical decision making has, as I said, wide ramifications. Take a case where promises are made to an employee in regards to compensation based on performance. These promises made are commitments and direct reflections of the integrity and ethics of the promise giver. If the leader who makes these promises then reneges on delivery of the promised compensation without cause, explanation or, worse yet, newly added caveats that were not part of the original equation, this behavior demonstrates very poor ethical decision making and harms the larger organization through the bad will created and potential loss of an asset to the team.

- <u>Expectations</u>

Moving beyond personal integrity and honesty is another very large area each follower must master: performance.

Performance is another critical aspect of followership. Performing well is the least tolerated level of performance you should allow for yourself as a follower learning the position or business. Chances are your leader/mentor expects excellent or better performance from you. Failing to perform to those expectations will wear down your leader/mentor's extended commitment to your progression, and cause your career movement to stagnate. Performing below expectations is never acceptable, even for a short time while learning a new skill or taking on larger responsibility than you previously held.

***Important Note:*** *Expectations are mentioned in several places throughout this book. Expectations are the most powerful force in the human universe. As such, this idea deserves respect from all of us. The power generated through expectations moves markets. If people expect the market to climb, chances are it will. If people expect the market to decline, chances are it will. If there is doubt about which direction the market should go, it will wobble–the predicament in 2006.*

*Expectations take us from the present state to the future state. Expectations are like tunnels through time. We set our alarm clock for tomorrow morning and expect it to go off and for us to begin a new day. This tunnel to the future assures us that there will be a future and that it will be OK. But if the clock doesn't go off and we wake up startled to see we are late, our entire day is shot–because our expectations were not met.*

*Another way of looking at it is to say that you hear about a great restaurant. You go there expecting the food to be great, only to discover it is very good, but it is not quite up to your expectations. Again, you failed to meet your expectations so were disappointed.*

Then take expectations into the workplace. Your leader expects you to complete an important report on time, but you miss the suspense. This provides the leader with the same feeling about your abilities as you felt when the food wasn't quite right at the restaurant. You are perceived as being ok, but not to be truly relied upon, just as you may return to that restaurant to eat, but probably won't because they just didn't quite get it right.

A primary task for leaders and followers is to establish clear expectations. Part of this clarity is mutuality in understanding. It does no good to state what you expect from someone if they are not allowed to voice either concern about the task or participate in the agreement. While there are always situations that do not allow this type of interaction, in general terms this is the best process.

Expectations mutually discussed and understood by both sides create mutuality in understanding and commitment to the expectations so clarified. From this point, you have no excuse for not meeting or exceeding expectations–and you know how important that is.

Beyond expectations delivery, performance demands a lot of you. It is how you are measured and evaluated. It is how many people are paid in a bonus-incented environment. In short, you have a huge amount of stock riding on your ability to demonstrate your performance to all the tasks you are assigned.

- Adaptability, Flexibility, Versatility

One aspect of your performance excellence is your adaptability. In business and life, change happens. How well do you adapt to the changes taking place? It is not so much as advertising you love change or that change does not affect you–both of which would make someone wonder about your internal honesty–as it is demonstrating through action that you do effectively engage and manage change.

Adaptability is very close to flexibility. Flexibility is a key to effectiveness. Being flexible means you do not breakdown or fail to act when change occurs, but look for opportunity and ability to continue and enhance the activity. Being adaptable means you can react in a way to take the change, embrace it, enhance it and succeed in the task through absorbing the new paradigm.

Adaptability and flexibility are completely the opposite of rigid. Being rigid in a fluid environment is counter-productive. Being rigid does not provide the leader with value, except in the case of a specific position that requires rigidity. Being rigid does not enable creative thinking. Creative thinking provides ideas, concepts and possibilities that can provide a potential spark of thought the leader can use to drive improvement.

Leaders need adaptable people. Effective followers must be prepared to accept diverse responsibility and excel in that new task. This ability to adapt to new environments, processes, responsibilities and maintain focus on purpose, process and team motivation is a critical self-control skill. Adaptability leads to our next topic, versatility.

Versatility differs from adaptability in that it covers the multi-skill aspect of performance. While being adaptable is a critical skill, versatility is a critical performance factor. If you are only able to do one or two things effectively, you are not versatile. It is important, from the leader's perspective, to have individuals who can effectively accomplish a multitude of tasks.

This versatility enables flexibility in assigning individuals to certain positions or roles. It ensures all the work required will be accomplished effectively, and frees the leader from worry about whether or not a certain task can be accomplished if a specific individual departs the team or is temporarily unavailable. With a team of versatile followers, the complementary nature of versatility ensures all tasks will be performed regardless of the mix of individuals.

Internally, being versatile builds confidence. The capability to perform a multitude of tasks in various settings or locations ensures you are an asset. Being able to chair a team, facilitate a strategy or project group, take over responsibility to manage an office or team, or any other task that comes at you, makes you an excellent resource.

- Credibility

The more you prove yourself to be able to do a multitude of tasks well, the higher your overall level of performance, the higher your level of adaptability and the more proven your integrity and honesty, the higher your level of credibility.

Credibility is vitally important in relational activities, because it brings with it a proven aura. When your perception is credible at the start, you can avoid spending the time it takes to establish credibility. Leaders need followers who take the time to build credibility. It provides a ready resource for input and support from a credible source. It provides a foundation for movement forward.

Credibility is vital not just for the purpose of your immediate team. Credibility is vital as a resource for corporate teams to be able to reach down to the field and get credible information. Credibility is vital for business or associations that span businesses. Credibility is vital for government, service sector organizations and the judicial system. Credibility is necessary for news organizations. In short, credibility is a must for any organization to operate effectively.

Credibility is a personal characteristic you create from within by controlling your own behavior and building a history of proven, credible actions. It is yours to build. It will only fall apart if you allow it to by falling away from the personal characteristic behaviors you had to embrace to gain credibility in the first place.

Taking steps to establish credibility entails following the path in all the items discussed to this point, and doing them well. Effective communication combined with honesty and integrity, combined with excellent performance in a multitude of tasks leads to your credibility.

• Energy

All of the tasks we have discussed require energy. How do you get energy? Energy is an intangible item that generates from within. Most of us can think of those people around us who clearly have no problem finding access to that infinite source of energy. We also know those people that appear tough to get excited or be energetic. For those individuals, it takes hard work to find energy.

Some people are natural energy springs. It is hard sometimes for these individuals to stop, evaluate and take the time to review or make a decision and then move on, because they are in constant motion. Coaching or leading these individuals is challenging, as the speed with which they take information, process it and get something back to you is so fast they seem to be ready for a new coaching before the old one is complete! Leaders who exhibit this behavior are hard to follow because they behave as if they expect everyone to be 16 hour a day motivated, and most people are just not.

Some people are natural dry springs. It is hard sometimes for these individuals to start, get moving, believe in the decision and make things happen, because they are motionless. Coaching or leading these individuals is hard, because it does not ever seem as if they take any coaching and apply it. You end up constantly asking them for feedback rather than hearing it without prodding. I do not recall ever seeing a leader who behaved in this manner. That says quite a lot about the role of energy in leadership. I have, however, seen managers in this role.

Most of us are in the middle. We can tap into our energy source but are not overwhelmed by it. We do not worry about not being able to be engaged because we do have access to enough energy to make things happen. This is one of the items that generate the appropriateness issue—as someone who can tap into energy gets "energized" because of a situation and rushes to respond based on that energized state.

• Attitude

Part of the internal energy we need to tap comes with our attitude. Working to be cognizant of all the behaviors necessary to demonstrate effective communication takes energy, but consciously working to be effective generates it—especially when you see your personal success through the direct affect on others because of your ability to effectively communicate.

Working to ensure you are cognizant of how you are perceived and ensuring you are maintaining a high level of honesty and integrity takes energy–but consciously working to charge these characteristics and live them generate it–especially when you see yourself portraying the role of credible leader you are striving to achieve. Both of these require a positive attitude.

A positive attitude can provide a deep source of personal motivational energy. Personal motivation is a key attribute. If you cannot motivate yourself, how do you expect to motivate others? Leaders need people who are optimistic, positive, energetic and able to share this with the team. A great task of followership is generating positive energy for the team as well as transferring positivity to the leader.

One of the key statements in life is that you cannot teach attitude. Someone's attitude is a true reflection of the internal processing within the person. Someone who is negative will be negative. While it is possible to work with someone to help them begin to change, it is truly more time consuming than most people have time for in the workplace.

Your attitude is yours. It is who you are. It is how you behave, talk, walk, think, listen, react, perform, motivate, influence, affect, plan, organize, spend, direct, lead; in short, your attitude is you because it affects everything about you.

It is for this reason that the traits of followership include attitude. As the owner of your own attitude, you have a choice. You can choose to maintain an attitude that is less than effective for personal or team success, or you can choose to modify your attitude, adapt the behaviors of effective communication and value, and demonstrate a changed positive attitude.

The second thing that is yours is your ability. Ability is inclusive of the tasks you can perform, such as communication and value behaviors and other skills we have discussed.

These two then, your attitude and your ability, equate to the summary of your person. It is on these two areas your access to growth, position and status hinge. A simple formula:

**Attitude + Ability = Access.**

You own and control two of the three. As a follower, you must focus and excel in these two areas you control. Your attitude and ability are your ticket to opportunity.

Leaders need people with a positive attitude and defined, excellent ability. These individuals are the people they want to give the access. These people inspire, motivate, perform admirably, ethically, are honest, and effectively communicate. In short, these are the future leaders.

- Commitment, Participation, Believability

No one accomplishes very much without commitment. Commitment is an internal choice and is directly in proportion to your attitude. Commitment is stepping over the edge of the precipice and acting on a belief that your parachute will open. Commitment is going forward with no reservations and no holding back. Commitment is energy, enthusiasm, determination, persistence and purpose, all rolled into one.

Effective followership demands commitment. Without commitment, you cannot demonstrate the actions or skills necessary to lead. Learning followership and being an effective follower demands your active engagement in supporting the leader.

Leaders need people who are committed to their team. Having effective follower's means the leader must devote less time on worry or observation of the team and more time on providing the mentoring, coaching and visioning demanded of a leader. This is another reason leaders like to see followers who participate.

Participation might sound like a small concept, but it is not. Followership excellence means active engagement with processes and people to enhance and improve. It means being on inter-departmental improvement teams. It means volunteering for additional work and committing time and energy to improve the entire team.

Lastly, there is a result of all of these skills, ideas, concepts and issues. The result is believability. Take everything about the person and summarize it into one idea. Are they believable or not? It is a simple question. It has only one of two potential answers. Either you are believable or you are not.

Believability is a critical summary. We evaluate people all the time. Do their actions match their words? Do they behave positively? Are they performing in a way a committed person would perform? Can they do everything they say?

Take everything you expect from an excellent follower and evaluate the performance. Does it match? Do they speak positively or complain? Do they talk behind peoples back? Do they bring ideas to the table, or just problems? Are they reliable or not?

We all use this simple litmus test constantly. Picture you are sitting in a conference room listening to someone talk, and their body language does not match their words. Believability–zero. Think about someone who says they do x and y consistently. You recall that on multiple occasions you observed the individual not doing x and y, contrary to their stated words. Believability–zero.

Employees at all levels must pass this test. It is not just a test of followership or leadership. This is a basic human performance issue. You can establish behaviors that bring believability to a high level. However, you must be on constant guard not to over commit and under deliver. The perception as non-believable is career limiting.

This is again, a demonstrated behavior. It is a leadership behavior, and a personal development behavior, as all of these are. Remember the idea is to mimic the behaviors of leaders and adapt them as your own. Leaders must be believed, or they cannot lead.

Personal characteristics are the touchstone of life. Success may be measured in many ways, but all will agree that success in personal behavior and demonstrating ethical value based characteristics equates to a life lived successfully, regardless of the position held.

For this reason, the goal to achieve high personal standards is not limited to a business or career focus. Rather, it is a life focus. As such, it should maintain a high primacy in your life for all your life.

## Followership Application:

As stated throughout this chapter, your personal character supports your ability to effectively lead and defines you as a leader. How then, do you ensure you have or develop the characteristics necessary for effective leadership?

This question truly ties directly to the argument that leadership is a natural talent and not a learned talent. If you naturally (through the ingrained behaviors you inherited biologically and the behaviors you learned as a child) behave in a perceived natural and effective/positive manner in communication and character issues, this process may seem easy to master. For those individuals, this book will provide excellent information for further clarification of their behaviors, and shed light on the task other individuals working to achieve leadership must pursue. In addition, it provides tools for developing future leaders you may be responsible to groom. However, what if this is not a natural process for you?

There are many reasons why character behavior is not necessarily a positive learned experience. What about someone who was born into a household of chaos? What about someone who was raised in a household where illegal activity was accepted as normal? What about someone who just simply had no positive role models while growing up? These individuals will find in this book some positive tools to help them overcome the lack of role models and a clear description and process for behavior demonstration that can lead to developed character and effective leadership.

One of the first things to accomplish, as usual, is to take an inventory. It is a simple reality that before you go anywhere, you must know where you are. Taking inventory is always a first step.

The difference is that character is not necessarily a demonstrated skill. Characteristics like honesty and integrity are not skills you demonstrate in the same manner as you demonstrate effective speaking. Therefore, to properly complete an inventory requires more than taking an assessment or questionnaire.

There are some psychological and behavior tests that can give you a good tendency inventory review. Several tests discuss your communication style through a series of questions. If you believe this would be beneficial for you, and it probably would be, I would suggest you take them.

The first true test of your character will be the discussions about personal characteristics and examples of good and bad behavior you need to have with your coach/leader. It may seem small, but it takes courage to talk about personal characteristics and behavior perceptions with your boss. It takes courage to admit you perceive ethical behavior differently.

In any case, the only place you can start in working to establish high level personal behavior characteristics is with your self and your leader/coach. Together, you must review behaviors, performance, decisions and actions not only for business applicability, but for your personal behavior as it related to each situation.

Most of what we determine is through what we observe. If a leader observes you make the right ethical decision and the two of you discuss it so she can review your thought process and finds it valid–then you are well on your way. However, if your leader sees you make an improper decision, you still must honestly discuss your motivations and thought process that brought you to the wrong conclusion.

This opens you up for your leader/coach to provide guidance and correction. This is the hard part, because most people do not want their internal decision making process to ever be questioned. However, to grow in character and modify your internal thought processes, you must be willing to do this. This choice to be open is the differentiator between someone who can change fundamentally and someone who cannot. If you do not, you cannot. If you cannot, you will fail.

For both natural and non-natural types, it is critical to demonstrate your character.

**Leadership Application:**

This is a very tough issue, as how you handle someone's personal character development or coaching can determine, to a very large extent, their commitment to the organization. This is a critical process in which how you do what you do is at least as important, if not more so, than what you do.

There are usually two types of individuals to work with in this area. The first are individuals who seem to get it and clearly demonstrate the personal characteristics you believe are necessary for effective business operations (natural). The second are individuals who apparently do not have the same value base as you represent (non-natural). There are unique challenges with each type of individual.

Additionally, in the scheme of coaching personal character, the focus should be on implications and ramifications from personal behavior, never on the value of the person you are coaching. Stick to the potential or real results that occur after a situation and discuss these as a way to discuss their personal characteristics. If you discuss their character directly, you run the risk of alienating, isolating, hurting and losing them.

This is another activity where you, the leader, demonstrate the behaviors you desire to have the follower mimic. As they see you behaving in an above board, consistent, empathetic and respectful manner, they will learn and grow. As they see your concern for the people who make up the business and how they perceive they are treated and led, they will learn and grow.

For the individuals who appear to be naturals, the tendency is to provide a little coaching and not too much oversight, because they are doing ok and no issues have occurred. You perceive them to be fitting in correctly and demonstrating the right characteristics. This is not the correct approach, because the natural needs as much reassurance of the rightness of their behavior as the non-natural. They need to see those same behaviors from the leader they will need to emulate as leaders when they work with future followers, whether natural or non-natural. To deny them this opportunity does not fully prepare them for this future role.

For the individuals who appear to be non-natural, the tendency is to provide too little coaching and too much oversight. This strange mixture seems to be based on the notion that someone who does not demonstrate the correct personal behavior characteristics cannot be salvaged, but must be watched to catch them making a poor decision so discipline can be provided until the time the individual is released from employment—or shifted to a non-growth position. This is obviously not the correct approach, because the non-natural who truly desires to learn and succeed is allowed to fall through the cracks. The non-natural who chooses not to succeed will choose to fail. Also, the successful non-natural needs to see the process you, the leader, follow, so they can find personal value in your commitment to them, and they can learn how to coach personal characteristics for future followers.

Keep foremost in your mind and plan the desired result–a productive team member with excellent communication skill built on a foundation of excellent personal character. This is the person you will charge with effectively executing your plan for success.

# 5

# *Execution Orientation*

Followership is not just about the personal, internal development process. Nor is followership concerned only with character and communication. Followership is about what you do with all your developed skills. What you do is perform. Followership then is about performance delivery and performance enhancement.

To be an effective follower you must be able to deliver results. Otherwise, you are a nice person, but you are just not necessary. No one wants to be unnecessary. In order to deliver results you have to deliver a high level of sustained execution in the day-to-day activities of the business. With this in mind, let us discuss execution orientation.

Execution is the ability to bring focus and organization to the people and process of the organization in order to deliver excellence in performance. That is the goal. This requires knowledge, observation, training, and motivation of your staff, in order to synergize their actions into a coherent, efficient and effective singular activity focused on mission success.

Execution demands an understanding of prioritization, joint action, synergy and desired outcome.

- This requires knowledge of the vision of the organization and its specific mission.

- This requires coordination and situational awareness skill in the creation of the required synergy.

- This requires visualization of the desired state and creating the pathways for the team to get there.

Execution is a summary word to describe a series of skills and attributes a follower must learn and enhance to achieve the effectiveness desired in a leader. Execution is not a passive skill. Execution is a very real application skill that describes your complete skill set in direct relation to the effective completion of the work at hand.

Operational tempo is another aspect of execution. Understanding the needs of the organization, the speed within which complex actions and decisions must be made to ensure the movement of activity is at the most efficient flow is critical.

All of this sounds highly complex, and it definitely can be. But in essence, execution is simply getting it done. Some people get so wrapped up in trivialities or things that are not important that they lose track of the need to keep focus on the important activities necessary for effective execution.

Are you able to perform the tasks required to be effective at your job? It's a simple question. And there is little room for argument. Either you can or you can't. If you can't, you have work to do. After all, how can you succeed in supporting your team if you cannot do your own job?

The ability to effectively do your job directly influences the level of respect your team has for you. It is critical for your team to develop respect for your skill. Otherwise, the ability you have to influence your team is diminished.

The primary role of supervision as it applies to followership is to influence your team to improve and sustain performance. Therefore, having the respect of your team through your ability to do your job is extremely important.

Performance is not a single issue for a supervisor or leader as it is for most workers. For most workers, performance is usually associated with a primary task. But for supervisors and leaders, it is much more. How you perform your critical job requirements is one thing. But also pay attention to how you perform your human interaction skills. How well you interact, show empathy and communicate with your team, peers and superiors will directly impact how your performance is perceived.

In this vein, make sure you are developing a balanced performance from the very start. Many people have a tendency to bust their butt in order to show how good they can perform, but burn themselves out in the process. That is not effective execution. Find the path that enables you to demonstrate excellence in business technical performance and excellence in human interaction performance, as well as balance with life. After all, you must have a time and place to go to recharge or you will burn out.

• Customer

The next step in execution is to have great customer focus. Why is it important to have great customer focus in the application of execution skill? Because the customer is the key to success, regardless of the business or service you are in. Without customers there is no business. Think about it. Where would your business be without customers?

Customers are the one's who bring in the revenue. Customers are the ones you must satisfy in order to keep them and continue to bring in their revenue. Even in the service industry, if you do not satisfy your customers, you will get bad reports and your service will be less acceptable or welcome than it could be. Even in government service, taking care of the customer is critical. No one wants legislators asking questions about the service provided to their constituents.

We cannot function in business without customers. As a follower, you must be customer focused.

- Are you aware of your customer's perception of the quality and delivery of your products?

- Are you engaged with your customers to the point of knowing their level of satisfaction?

- Are you doing everything you can to ensure your customers receive the best products or services and remain loyal customers?

Followership demands you focus on your customers and ensure your team delivers the products and services in a way and at a price that satisfies them, while meeting the needs of your business.

I'm sure you have heard the phrase, "If you don't take care of your customer, someone else will." This is entirely true. How does this tie into execution? Without customer focus, the performance delivered serves no purpose other than increasing costs. Because if customers are not there to buy your products, all you are doing is increasing inventory. That is not effective execution.

*I was a member of a bank. I had a checking and savings account with this organization, and I used their on-line banking services. One day, I went to the bank to cash a check. The bank tellers were just talking among themselves and not really paying any attention to those of us in line. A few days later, I had reason to go to the bank again. And again, I met the same behavior—even to the extent that some of the other customers were grumbling about this big corporate bank and how they never felt like a real member anymore.*

*About two weeks later, I had another similar experience, so I went and found a local bank that truly wanted my business. I still bank with them, because they take care of the customer.*

*When I went into the first bank to close my accounts, the lady simply smiled and took care of the transactions. It was only after everything was done and my accounts were closed that I said to her how strange that no one even asked why I was closing my accounts. She kind of looked at me a moment, and then said, well, why are you closing your accounts?*

*I pointed to the poster on the wall behind her, and said that is why. The poster said, "If you don't take care of the customer, someone else will." This organization failed me, and probably others, simply because the culture was allowed to develop where the customer truly was not job one. Because of that their costs increased, as their revenue decreased. Maybe my little account wasn't big enough to be important, but I was a customer, just not important enough for them.*

Another critical set of customers is your staff, co-workers and superiors. They are as critical for the success of your mission as anyone else. Too often the people we need to get the job done to support the external revenue generating customers are overlooked as to their true value. If in your execution process role you do not consider the value of your internal customers and how best to support and utilize their skills, your ability to deliver excellence to external customers diminishes.

- Details, Big Picture, Conciseness

Another significant aspect of execution is to pay attention to the details. How many times have you seen something, such as a pamphlet or presentation, where there was a mistake? It is true that the majority of the presentation is perfect. However, that small error is glaring.

If you are not performing your job to the highest level, you probably do not know all aspects of the job. If you are not performing in this manner, you are not truly capable of watching the quality of the performance. If you are not observing and inspecting the quality of the performance, you are not showing concern for the customer. This attention to detail impacts many aspects of your performance and your team's performance. It is a critical learning.

Attention to detail does not only mean you dot the "I's" and cross the "T's". It means you pay attention to attitudes, processes and how the process is working. There is a lot of detail to observe in the performance of business. There is great detail in each individual's performance on the team. There is great detail in how the team is interacting together to synergize and improve overall output.

This is not to say you should be so focused on the details that you cannot see the bigger picture. In essence, the big picture is also a detail that you must see. It is a tapestry of interrelated action, constantly shifting and changing, that you must master to fully be an effective follower, owner or leader.

This is not as easy to accomplish as it may seem. It takes training and effort to observe details at multiple levels.

Closely related to detail orientation is the ability to be concise. What does this mean? Let me give you an example of someone who was not concise.

*I worked for a manager one time that just couldn't get to the point. She would talk around a subject forever. Sitting in a meeting, when she began talking, you could see people's eyes roll up and minds shut down, as they knew they would be listening to "stuff" for an inordinate amount of time, with no clear purpose.*

This is classic inability to be concise. Being concise means just the opposite, as you are able to sift through the multitude of pieces of data and information about a topic and bring it down to a few lines. This is a definite execution skill, as it enables you to bring closure to complex items and move the team or process forward. Being concise takes ambiguity and confusion out of the process and provides clarity and brevity in discussion.

Followership demands you learn to be concise. As you see larger performance trends develop, look to understand what the key drivers of that performance are. Look to see if you can bring the overall issue down to a few lines.

*For example, a situation in which overall productivity has declined slowly over a period of time develops. When you go into the meeting, there is no need to take the time to go over the reports of performance and why it is an impact, etc. Instead, be prepared to bring it down to a basic, concise statement. Something like: "Productivity decreases are a direct reflection of the overtime increase we have experienced, due to higher turnover than anticipated, which is causing increased quality errors and re-work."*

That type of a statement states the problem, establishes a direct symptom and a direct cause for the symptom that is driving the performance. Of course, ensure you always have data to validate your statements.

In this manner, you are demonstrating execution orientation in that you see the issue and understand its cause. Being able to clearly speak in a concise manner greatly helps the team drive to the source of the issue without undue delay or wasted time.

- Competence & Directing

Of course, you cannot be concise or perform your job or be respected by your team if you are not competent. Probably the biggest visible perceived trait of anyone is their level of competence.

Competence is a basic evaluative concept we all apply to anyone in any position beneath us, around us or above us. Competence is an evaluation of someone's ability to perform all the roles they are assigned. Competence is also deeply related to how you do your job.

Have you ever heard someone described as incompetent? Being labeled incompetent is a funeral march for leadership. Whenever someone is labeled incompetent, it is a signal that they have demonstrated failure in multiple areas.

Competence is a goal to strive to achieve. You must constantly work to ensure you know the job, understand the tasks, establish sound human interaction and be naturally positive. Competence is a concept we bestow upon those whom we perceive are able to get the job done in an effective manner. Getting the job completed in an effective manner means accomplishing the task through positive interaction and application of influence.

Competence is an energy booster. Incompetence is an energy drainer. If people perceive you are incompetent, they will not give you the energy and support you need for success, because they have determined that you will not be successful. This can become a self-fulfilling prophecy.

As you grow through each of these levels, you arrive at a place where in order to execute the business, you must direct action. If you are not competent and viewed as such by your team, your direction may be questioned. After all, let's say someone has been doing their job for a while and know it very well, and then along comes a new supervisor who clearly doesn't seem to get it, and he tells you to do something that you know is totally not right. Do you do it? Or do you go talk to his supervisor to get the issue resolved? Chances are that whatever you do, it is not following the directions as given.

Therefore, as the new supervisor, you must be competent to provide direction. You must build cohesion with your team. You must deliver a consistently competent performance in order to be allowed to influence. Bottom line, if you want to direct actions effectively to support the execution of your business, you must be competent in your job.

Additionally, directing action requires knowledge of the jobs of everyone you are responsible for, how they interact with each other and other sections, units, departments or agencies, and how these actions will impact the customer and financial performance. Directing actions are critical and necessary, but must be weighed against potential error from wrong decision.

- <u>Affecting Positive Change</u>

There are several attributes or skills necessary to effectively execute, and in this chapter we discuss several of them. This is not a totality discussion of execution orientation. However, suffice to say that as you courageously apply the communication skill you are developing on a base of solid character behavior, you must take action. That action is behavior based and summarized in a word—performance. Your task is not only to perform well, but also to excel in performance through solid and consistent execution.

Execution then refers to action. Before you can take action you must know the context within which you operate. You must know the parameters of the position you hold, the mission of the team or group you are in, the processes and business goals, and the direction provided by the leader.

This basic knowledge usually comes from previous experience, the positions held prior to promotion, experience from previous employers, job training and education. The very small bubble wherein you have control is the first place you must review your execution orientation.

Ask yourself some questions.

- Are the processes I am responsible for as efficient as they can be?

- Are the people under my responsibility fully trained?

- Is my team generating the expected revenue?

- Are my costs in line with expectations?

- Do all of my team members know what is expected of them?

- Am I fully competent to provide the coaching necessary for my team?

These are not all the questions you need to ask, but you should get the idea.

- You need to dig down several layers to understand who, what, where, why and how of the performance for everything within your control.

- You must know if it meets expectations or not.

- You must know why it does or does not meet expectations.

- You must know what action is necessary to improve or sustain this performance to expectations.

- You must know where synergy for your team is strong and where it is weak.

- You must know the weakest and strongest link in your area.

Knowing all there is to know in your area provides you the basis for affecting positive change. If you do not know what the actual problem is, you cannot affect positive change. You will affect change, but then you will have to wait and see if it was positive or not.

Affecting positive change in your area of control clearly demonstrates your ability to execute. Leaders need people who can analyze and evaluate effectively. Leaders need people who can provide targeted solutions to complex problems, create the change necessary to affect the problem and move the team toward success. This is execution orientation.

After you have learned your area of control, you shift your awareness to other areas. One area for a larger organization is the corporate organization. In order to be effective in your business you need to have high organization knowledge.

- Organization knowledge is knowledge of who, what, where, when, why and how for your organization.

- It is knowledge of who to talk with about specific issues.

- It is knowledge of how to maneuver within the organization for greatest effectiveness and efficiency.

- It is knowledge of how to coordinate, as protocols must be followed in many cases.

These steps of organizational knowledge tie directly into the ability to affect change through effective relationship management. If you do not take the time to develop any relationships with the people you will need to work with, you create limitations on your ability to affect change for your team. Contrarily, as you build good relationships with the people you need to work with, you gain support, insight, ideas and energy that will help you as you work to affect positive change.

These relationship building opportunities cannot be taken for granted or ignored. Failure to build relationships with other leaders in the organization limits your ability to act for your team, and therefore limits the organizations ability to perform effectively in the marketplace. This is not effective execution. There is a direct connection between your ability to affect change, your organizations execution effectiveness, and the relationships you participate in across the organization. No one stands alone, outside of or above this symbiotic organizational truth.

- Business Knowledge

Another thing you will find in any organization is an overall purpose of vision. Most organizations have a vision. If you do not know the vision of the organization, how do you expect to focus your abilities to achieving the vision? How will you know if you are going in the right direction?

Knowing the CEO's perspective, reading company literature, establishing a personal connection with the leadership, and especially, working with your mentor/leader, are all effective tools for understanding the purpose of the organization. Through knowing this purpose you learn how you fit into this team. It is very important to ground yourself in the team. If you continuously know where you fit in, you consistently know what is expected from you, both formally and informally. However, if you do not know where you fit in, you continuously question yourself, remain in uncertainty, and your effectiveness is reduced. Talk with your leader/coach about this to clarify your place on the team.

The organizational structure also provides a glimpse into the purpose of the organization, as well as the executable direction of the organization. Learning the key players and establishing communication with them helps you not only when you really need help, but also places you in a position as participant and pro-active member. This will distinguish you from many others, but more than that, it enables you to learn about the team and continue self-growth.

Leaders need people who focus on becoming participants in the team. Leaders need people who are pro-actively learning and establishing connections. Followership demands you know, in as great of detail as possible, the organization you are part of. Your overall goal is to be highly executable, knowing the team will assist you as you move to enhance your performance dynamics. Knowing the supporting organization is very important. However, knowing the business is critical.

Execution cannot happen in an environment where the business is not known. As stated above, you have a requirement to know the area you control. There are issues larger than your control area that tie directly to the business you are part of, such as the business in regards to the technical understanding and knowledge of your industry.

Ask yourself some questions.

- What are the specific opportunities and threats in the industry?

- What are the strengths and weaknesses of my business unit?

- What are the innovations in the industry?

- What will be the impact of new entrants in the industry?

- How well does my business unit perform?

- What is my margin?

- Are my costs in line with industry standards?

- Can I reduce costs without reduction of production capability, quality or negative morale impact?

- Must I reduce costs regardless?

You must ask yourself hundreds of questions. You must strive to be the subject matter expert in your business. Followership demands business knowledge, and execution cannot happen effectively without it.

- Decisiveness & Sound Judgment

As you develop the skills of followership, you are learning the full expectation of ownership. Full ownership means you know the business, because your career, your employee's future and your employer's organization depend on your sound judgment.

A prelude to sound judgment, however, is the demonstrable skill of decisiveness. Leaders need people who can evaluate information, understand the constraints of choice, and yet make effective, timely decisions. Decisiveness does not mean you make a decision because you can. It also does not mean you make a decision because you should. Nor does it mean you make a decision recklessly, because you think a decision must be made right now.

Decisiveness means you build the decision-making skill up through trial and error into a consistent pattern of behavior. This pattern of behavior demonstrates a tendency to make effective decisions in a timely manner. Consistently asking your leader/mentor if x is the right decision before you make the decision is not decisiveness.

There are times when you must and should have conversation about the ramifications of a decision. There are questions that must and should be asked of concerned parties to validate the decision is necessary, applicable and required. However, after all the questions have been asked and the data is available, the decision must be made. There is a time for questions, but there is a natural time for a decision.

How many times have you been in a situation where all the information that is going to be available is there; yet the person responsible to make the decision does not act? It is an awkward time for all, not least for the indecisive leader. Understanding this process, gaining an understanding of the rhythm of timing and demonstrating a clear ability to make decisions is critical for growth into ownership. If you cannot make decisions effectively, why would anyone desire to place you in an ownership position over their business?

Obviously, no one would. This skill is critical for response to change. Change in the information overloaded world of today happens so fast it takes your breath away. The inability to make decisions clearly then, becomes a major skill requirement. This decisiveness skill leads directly to sound judgment, because the true question above is about the cumulative decision making ability of the person.

Sound judgment is a personal characteristic that relates directly to effective execution. This trait is a summary of decisions. It is an evaluative perspective on the rightness of the choices you make in regards to all decisions you are required to make, as well as the recommendations and suggestions you provide. It is a cumulative evaluation of your common sense.

We do not take a test or make one decision and have the label of sound judgment bestowed upon us. Rather, it takes time to earn this recognition. It is vital to be labeled as someone who demonstrates sound judgment, because this demonstrates your perceived future or increasing value to the team and organization. Leaders need people who demonstrate sound judgment.

- <u>Management & Problem Solving</u>

A large part of execution involves effective process, data, procedural, financial and system management. One of the most important aspects of followership is learning effective management. Managing is a key skill that every follower must master. Leaders need people who can clearly manage processes, performance metrics and ensure business processes are followed. Managing involves scheduling people for work, analyzing costs, revenue and budgets, measuring and analyzing quality and implementing correction as needed. In short, management is all about the business process and application of process to ensure effectiveness.

You will spend countless hours reviewing these managed processes. Your leader/coach will spend countless hours discussing these and the ramifications and interconnectedness of various processes. As a follower desiring to demonstrate effective execution, you must learn and demonstrate effective management.

However, this book is not about management. This book is about growing leadership. To be a leader you must have expertise in effective management concepts. You demonstrate your ability every day as you demonstrate decisiveness in your area of responsibility and perform above standard. You show your management skill as you establish measurement processes, analyze results and implement corrective action. You show how well you manage through effective time and task management.

Leaders need effective managers. Effective managers get the vast amount of work in organizations accomplished. Creating effectiveness in your personal skill provides your leader with a pillar to lean on and a true resource to draw upon.

Followership demands effective management. To be a great follower means you demonstrate the ability to manage your skill development process. If you cannot effectively manage your own development process, can you be relied upon to manage the development of other individuals and a business unit? Learning followership skill demonstrates your personal growth and management effectiveness. It brings you up to a higher level of performance and prepares you for the next aspect of growth.

However, before we move to the next chapter, there is one final word about execution orientation. One of the key execution skills you must master is the ability to solve problems. Problem solvers are a unique breed. Many people walk in the door with problems. It is not too hard to identify things that are not going exactly right. The hard part, for many people, is to identify a resolution to the problem and bring that with them when they bring the problem.

Problem solvers provide several things. First, they demonstrate their ability to identify problems. Second, they demonstrate their ability to analyze and think critically. Third, they demonstrate their ability to evaluate a potential resolution for the problem. Lastly, they provide their leader/mentor with the opportunity to praise and coach.

Having someone walk in with a problem/solution is a wonderful opportunity to reinforce positive behavior and effective thought process. It is also a great opportunity to teach someone something new, all in a positive manner based upon positive behavior. Problem solvers demonstrate initiative. Initiative demonstrates commitment. Commitment leads to ownership.

In closing, remember that execution orientation is application focused. It is not an internal development of character. It is not an internal evaluation of skill. Quite the contrary, execution orientation is the focus a follower must have to effectively execute all the processes, programs, actions, activities, people, resources and plans in such a manner as to synergize the operation for maximum effect. Anything less is not execution orientation.

## Followership Application:

Execution can seem like an insurmountable obstacle. Execution demands you learn everything, make correct decisions in a timely manner; motivate, collaborate, synergize, evaluate and deliver excellence through the application of skill involving other people. However, remember that these expectations do not occur in a vacuum, nor do they occur overnight.

Like speaking, the chances of being asked to speak to a group about a subject you know nothing about are extremely remote. With execution, the chances of being placed in a position you know nothing about and expected to perform to a high level are remote. The problem with many of our development processes, however, is that we expect high performance with too little coaching and guidance—which is a fundamental subject this book addresses.

Your ability to execute, therefore, has not occurred in a vacuum. You have been actively working to execute by taking these steps:

- You are now working to learn and mimic effective communication. In this process, you have been establishing relationships with the team, learning strengths and weaknesses and building trust.

- You have been demonstrating positive personal characteristics, which enable the trust you are building to grow, enable people to buy in to your new role and begin to create team synergy.

- You have taken the time to learn all there is to know about your business unit or area of responsibility. You know how it works, who does what, why things are done as they are, etc. In short, you have become a technical expert in your area.

Execution, then, is based on the application of what you know and practice, using effective communication to lead, direct, coach and guide the team based on a foundation of character to deliver high performance. There are multiple approaches to establishing execution as an internal process. The one I have found to be most effective follows.

1. Take the time to write down your evaluation of the processes and people you are becoming responsible for. Write down your thoughts, positives, negatives, potential coaching, process changes, actual observed performance and behavior, etc. Write out in a logical format any observations or reasons you perceive that your team, process or unit is not executing as well as it could, should or must.

2. Having taken the time to organize your thoughts in a comprehensive manner, sort through them and prioritize the major stumbling blocks for effective execution. This prioritization may not be by most important to least important. It may be by greatest impact to least impact. Get a good quality process book. Read and understand how to use the various tools available, such as Force Field Analysis, Cause and Effect (Fishbone) Diagram, Pareto Chart, Histograms, Run Charts, and other tools. Many organizations provide training specifically on quality tools. If yours does, take the class. If not, talk with your leader on the best way for you to get up to speed in this area. Nothing replaces analysis in determining where true errors occur.

3. Having prioritized your analysis into the primary issues you perceive, based on fact, to be preventing your team from executing effectively, begin to brainstorm potential resolutions. Often, the best suggestions come from the people involved with the execution of the process, so get your team together and discuss these issues (depending on your specific situation, it is usually best to discuss holding these meetings with your leader/coach first.) This is a true test of your emerging leadership. This also can be extremely productive in team building and performance enhancement.

4. After you have decided on your suggested resolutions to your identified issues, present them to your leader for open, honest discussion. Do not be surprised if your leader disagrees with your conclusions. After all, you are learning to be a leader; you are demonstrating followership and just beginning to step into the bounds of ownership. At this stage, however, you are still relatively new to the

entire process. You leader will fully appreciate your initiative, energy, problem identification and suggested resolutions, not only because they may just work, but because they provide an excellent opportunity to provide you the coaching and feedback you need to continuously grow.

5. After this discussion, you should have some tangible items to implement in order to improve the execution of the team. The last piece of execution then, is effective change implementation and management. It is only half the ball game to identify issue or resolutions. It is the other half to apply your learning and positively affect change. This is execution.

As the follower learning the ropes, you need to be pro-active in searching for problems and solutions. You need to be actively engaged in demonstrating your commitment to do what it takes for success. This is not a day job, but a life style choice. You are on the verge of becoming accountable for your teams performance and applied ownership. Without building effective execution skill, you will have a tough time demonstrating the ownership necessary to step up to be the leader.

## Leadership Application:

It becomes ever more critical for the leader to fully engage in the development process for the follower. While it is critical for you to complete assessments, develop plans and observe/provide feedback on communication skill; and while it is critical for you to observe and discuss character development; it is even more critical to move beyond those initial development processes to the establishment of effective execution skill in your followers.

Many people are not exposed to execution. They perceive that coming to work and doing their job is execution. However, just doing your job is not execution, it is an important part of it, but it is only part of it.

As a leader you must demonstrate the skills of execution, coach and develop those skills in others, and clearly demonstrate the positive affect execution has on performance delivery.

One of the items necessary for your followers to effectively execute is a thorough understanding of applied analysis. This quality evaluation of performance is critical for your followers to be able to effectively analyze their area of responsibility, evaluate performance against expectation, determine where breakage exists, and provide recommendations and follow-up.

One problem with this is that not everyone has attended training or received an education in application of these tools. Therefore, it provides a good opportunity for you to provide this training to your followers, schedule training for them, or discuss their experience with quality measurement if they come with this knowledge. In all cases, this gives you an opportunity to level set your followers to ensure they are at or above a minimal threshold of understanding.

As you evaluate your follower's performance, ask to see their documentation of performance they are using to evaluate. Is it thorough? Is it complete? Have they applied the right tool for the right reason? Have they reached good conclusions? Is there more to the substance of the issue than they fully appreciate? How can you effectively coach for improvement in this area? What are their strengths and weaknesses in the analysis process? Are there personnel or financial implications they have not taken into account?

The list of questions goes on. Your job is both to ensure the business, process or area the follower is gaining responsibility for is performing and executing effectively AND develop the follower as they begin to assume more accountability and ownership for that performance.

As stated earlier, how you do what you do is as important as what you do. In this case, as in many others, the art of coaching and leadership you demonstrate will say more than the words you use. You must be an effective executor yourself before you can teach anyone else how to execute. You must demonstrate effective communication skill yourself before you can teach anyone else how to communicate. You must demonstrate excellent personal character yourself before you can coach someone else on their character.

The application of execution is the most critical final step for the follower. Their progression begins with effective communication, is grounded in personal character, and takes on technical expertise to effectively execute which should lead to enhanced and sustained performance, baring unforeseen circumstances. All of this has been accomplished through your coaching and under your wing. They have begun to feel responsibility, but as of yet you have not shifted over accountability or ownership for that performance. Once they demonstrate effective execution, they are ready for the next step to leadership.

# 6

## *Developing Ownership*

Up until now, we have primarily focused on internal skill development and individual performance outside of the accountability sector.

- By now, a follower should have established and demonstrated excellent communication skill, positive personal character behavior and effective execution performance.

- By now, a follower should be confident of his or her abilities and is no longer fearful of providing their perspective on issues.

- By now, a follower is beginning to sense and taste the energy of accountability and is ready to take it to a higher level.

- By now, the leader should have a very good sense of the strengths and opportunities of their follower.

- By now a leader would have evaluated, coached and developed communication skills to ensure the follower could be effective.

- By now the leader should have determined the character of the follower and coached where necessary to ensure the follower established and strengthened their positive character traits.

- By now the leader should be ready to begin the process of fully energizing their follower and enabling their transcendence to leadership.

In order to take it to a higher level we need to establish a new understanding. As in building a strong structure, you first dig the pilings deep for support and then you build the framework on top of it that will support the structure. Ownership (framework) is built on followership (pilings) that will support leadership (structure).

You have already begun the journey to ownership. As stated above, you are at a threshold where you have a choice to step up to a higher level. It is not a position change or a new title that puts you on this path. It is not a different degree of responsibility. The path you are embarking on–excellence in leadership—is deeper than that and goes to the heart of the transformation to leadership. The transformation from follower to leader goes through a transcendence called ownership.

• Ownership

Ownership begins with the self. You must analyze your self and make the decisions necessary to hone your personal behaviors and skill to a deeper or higher level. If you fail to take this singularly critical ownership step, it is doubtful you will be successful in your leadership endeavor. This is simply because the discipline necessary to create the causation of positive growth will elude anyone that does not first begin on the inside.

Once the step of internal ownership is made and the skills are moving towards excellence, the greater behavior of ownership can begin. This next step is critical as well, because if you do not take your internal actualization and focus it toward external behavior demonstration, you miss the potential for leadership of a team.

Ownership is the catalyst necessary to move the follower into a deeper commitment and higher growth toward leadership. Taking the skills of followership and charging them with ownership enables the follower to transcend to leadership.

All this sounds simple enough, but it is a very complex process, that begins, as stated above, with internal discipline. It is simple in that it appears to be a singular item that generates transcendence. It is complex in that ownership is not a single item, it is also many interrelated items, such as self discipline, responsibility, accountability and energy. Let's begin the discussion with self discipline.

• Self Discipline

Self discipline is potentially the single greatest achievement of commitment for the individual. It is easy to go along to get along. It is easy to just do enough to get by. It is easy to barely achieve when your goals and expectations are low.

However, when you desire to be the best you can be, you must begin with your self. The road to self achievement is filled with potholes of distraction and paths that are easy. However, if you allow other people, requirements or needs to distract you from the real work of growth that self discipline requires, or if you take the easy paths to your goal, you will soon discover that you have gotten nowhere.

Self discipline is hard. This is not just telling yourself you need to not eat that candy bar today. This is defining your growth needs, working to understand what you need to improve through internal evaluation and external feedback. This is using your mind as an analytical tool and your heart as a generator of energy and power, and digging deep into your soul to synergize them into a single focused thought–control of self to the point of ownership over the choices the self makes.

If you think this is easy, you do not understand how deep this goes. True self discipline is a life transforming event. Most people never experience this level of awareness. Most people are disciplined in moderate ways or for short periods of time.

However, true self discipline becomes the compass that guides you through life. Synergizing the core of your self into a purposeful direction is a truly rewarding experience. Success creates a causation that remains within.

In the development of ownership, this causation of discipline reaches the well of energy that resides deep within. It is in the tapping of this unlimited energy source that you find the drive to support the self discipline through inner power and strength. It is also in this well of energy you find the charge and motivation to raise to leadership.

As you begin to harness this inner strength, you will begin to expand your skills and knowledge. In addition, you will begin to take on responsibility.

- Responsibility

Responsibility is something you develop from an early age. You learn responsibility for your actions as you grow. Everything from having to clean your room to put away your toys has taught you responsibility. Having to turn in assignments in school and get homework complete teaches responsibility. In short, the journey through life is filled with responsibility. Paying your bills, obeying the law, managing your household budget–everything teaches and reinforces the basic idea of individual responsibility.

The significant difference now, is that the responsibility you have is not just for your personal behavior or performance, but also for other people in a larger team. Once you entered the process of followership you began expanding your area of responsibility. You now are responsible for both your personal actions and that of a team. Accepting and performing well under this changed circumstance is a solid step forward.

Learning to accept responsibility for a team or process involving more than just your self is a difficult step. There is no sugar pill you can take that will make this new role all sweetness and light; contrarily, you will experience the thrill of achievement and the thrill (or agony) of failure. The key to this point is that you have a greater opportunity to make mistakes and learn without having the full accountability for the failure placed squarely on your person. However, you should have felt the weight of responsibility on your shoulders, as this is stepping up into the accountability role you must accept if you will transcend into leadership.

Finally, however, you must begin taking proactive energetic responsibility for the actions of each member of the team. You are now the subject matter expert. You are now coaching and motivating. You have begun to establish solid relationships. You are working to ensure the team achieves performance goals. In short, you have initiated a commitment to the people you support and you are supported by. This is the last step toward ownership.

This is also why you must have self discipline. These activities will test your ability to remain focused, positive and think. Without the internal motivation of your personal energy source, it will be tough.

Now let's talk about the behaviors that you should exemplify. Behaviors that demonstrate responsibility in ownership are behaviors that accept responsibility for the performance of individuals within your owned space. In this ownership space are the processes and people your specific followership behavior affects. This does not require you to be designated owner of a certain business unit. Quite the contrary, you demonstrate effective ownership through informal behaviors as well.

This process is easier and clearer if you are a designated team, process or business unit manager. As such, ownership can be more easily visualized as the sphere of processes and people you directly control. Having this control, you must demonstrate the followership characteristics as defined in previous chapters. Your ability to effectively communicate, built on a foundation of character, supported by execution, with courage to do the right and necessary thing, directly and positively influences those within your sphere towards excellence. Internalizing the self discipline necessary to remain focused and on task while tapping your internal energy leads into acceptance of responsibility for this process in a pro-active manner by ensuring full engagement in the process that leads to a responsible level of ownership.

Responsibility through ownership is a greater depth of responsibility. It is accepting and embracing responsibility as a means of achieving excellence, not as a statement of position. You can sum up accountability for a process in a chart. You cannot sum up the ownership of the responsibility to sustain the process to the most effective means possible and proactively monitor, modify and act, in a chart.

This type or ownership responsibility springs from followerships commitment to growth. Learning behaviors and knowledge of effective communication, seeking internal spiritual enlightenment and development of the highest personal attributes, being execution able and acting courageously raise you above normal responsibility. These attributes, when empowered with self-actualized ownership, bring you within mere moments of leadership.

Leaders need owners who take responsibility for the business as if it were their own. Leaders know these individuals will enable the overall team to rise above mediocrity to success.

Ownership demands responsibility. How can you own anything if you do not take responsibility? How can you truly be responsible for anything if you do not behave as if or feel you own it? Ownership and responsibility cannot be separate from each other. They should not be. Rather, they need to combine in positive supported ways to ensure the follower begins to transcend followership to leadership.

• Accountability

Adding to responsibility is accountability. Accountability in ownership again transcends accountability found in an organization chart. Accountability in ownership must be such that it is a welcome energizer. Ownership accountability behaviors must clearly demonstrate acceptance of and thriving positive power gained through accountability.

As with responsibility, accountability is more than your specific, documented accountability for x. It is accepting and taking accountability for people's behaviors, performance generation, quality, attitudes, coaching, humanity and all aspects of the business within your sphere. Accountability in this vein of ownership is acknowledgement and acceptance that you are accountable for more than the organization chart depiction.

Being accountable at this level creates a causation of excellence. This causation drives positive attitude energy, process modification, and people skill enhancement and performance improvement. This causation is the driver for transcendence from following to leading. Without accepting accountability for all you are accepting ownership for, you cannot move forward to lead.

This high-energy passion for movement forward is the desired state of ownership. This is where you must dig deep inside to find the courage to separate your self from others as you strive to achieve. You can no longer be satisfied with the status quo. You now move into owning the input and results of all the activities in your sphere. This level of ownership takes focused energy. Without the courage and conviction of your personal commitment, you cannot achieve this.

This desired state reflects itself through you in your behaviors. This ownership state requires your effective application of followership at a higher level of personal investment. The personal investment you choose to make is the separator for many people over whether they will move on to leadership or remain an effective team member, but not leader.

Many people do not want to move beyond being a follower. That is ok as well. Not everyone will become a leader. Some people will show some leadership characteristics through the followership characteristics they develop. Some will move into positions of technical leadership, but not raise high for fear of failure–interpreted as fear of ownership.

This desired state is not for everyone, but as you move through this acceptance and make this commitment, you will find new strength and energy in your quest of leadership. Acting within this desired state is both high stress and high reward, but primarily it is high energy. Someone who takes energy from others cannot move through this process, as true ownership understands the need to energize others to greatness.

- Internalizing Ownership

Ownership is a natural extension of life. All animals have territory. This is a natural phenomenon. Humans also follow this trend of establishing territory. A step inside this process reveals that we demonstrate ownership over those things we claim territory over. If we own it, we are free to make decisions about it. Contrarily, if we do not own it, we know we are not supposed to make decisions about it.

Ownership is about clarifying this natural state concerning the processes, procedures and confusion in life and business. Once you understand what you are truly the owner of, you can then act freely and proactively in the furtherance of this owned estate. The removal of confusion and chaos in business can be attributed to removal of confusion of ownership.

Developing internal ownership is the single most difficult issue for many people and organizations. It causes the individual to make a choice. Do you want to step out into the void of owning something that might fail, or do you want to remain safe and secure where you are? It causes organizations to make a choice as well. Do we want control centrally to minimize potential mistakes or can we empower people in the field and support them effectively?

- Followership prepares you to take the step.

- Leadership demands you take the step.

- Ownership is the step.

Organizations experience this same phenomenon because organizations are followers and leaders experiencing the exact same issues on a different scale. There is tension from the bottom to the top and top to bottom of organizations. This is not necessarily bad, as the energy derived from tension is a huge multiplier of energy for the organization. The key is to ensure the energy is focused and positive by removing roadblocks that prevent individuals from being able to fully contribute.

This is an organizational ownership issue. As we discuss individual ownership, it must be recognized that if the leaders of the organization do not enable, trust or allow their followers or subordinate leaders to own their piece, they disrupt the positive energy flow necessary for followership and leadership development.

Obviously, the business unit leader at any level does not solely own and manage the unit at his or her discretion. It is a shared ownership and shared responsibility for the entire leadership team.

*For example, let us say there are 12 teams, Team A–L, each with 15 individuals and one leader. The 12 leaders are co-equal. They are divided into three larger teams, each with a leader, Leader 1—3. These three leaders, in turn work for a single leader, Leader Z, who in turn works for someone, up to the point of reporting to shareholders.*

*In this scenario, the Team Z leader is responsible and accountable for the performance of this unit. Obviously, Leader 1 is responsible for the performance of the entire Leader 1 team, which includes four smaller teams. The ownership issue is one of scale and appropriateness. Leader A is accountable for the performance of the 15 person team, but cannot decide, at his or her discretion, to pay them more, hire more than necessary, slow down production, etc., on his own. His ownership is in meeting or exceeding expectations and achieving business goals within acceptable business practices.*

*Each level in the chain of ownership experiences ownership for items, processes and performance in differing degrees. The key is to ensure processes are built in such a manner that individuals do feel this ownership. If, in the example above, Leader 1 constantly tells Leader A, B and C what to do, micro-manages them and does not give them an opportunity to actively contribute, the overall performance of the responsibility area of Leader 1 will decline.*

*However, if Leader 1 strengthens each Leader and creates a sense of ownership for each one, the sum of the three parts excelling in performance will be far greater than the sum of the three as unproductive, non-owners stuck in a process. Moreover, this performance will have an opportunity to synergize and perform at an even higher rate, potentially to deliver what four or possibly five moderate teams could achieve.*

- When people believe they have a true stake in the organization and feel a sense of worth, they stick.

- Ownership reduces turnover, enhances morale and performance and delivers consistently higher returns.

- It does no good to recruit for the best only to treat them like non-team members or micro-manage them into the ground.

- Energy is the key; the positive focused energy of ownership is the largest advantage any organization has.

- At the individual level, this is the difference between delivering excellence and delivering mediocrity.

- Tell someone they do not have a stake in things, and that their opinion really does not matter and you will definitely receive the return on investment you make.

- The opposite is also true. Give someone a true voice and a stake in the process, and coach, train and mentor them effectively, and they will deliver to the highest standard.

Also at the individual level, there is the difference between the natural leader and the developed leader.

- The natural leader has the tendency to take responsibility and behave in a way that appears to be one based on understanding of ownership.

- The developed leader works through the skills to a point at which a decision inside must be made to become a leader.

The natural leader may have skills that are similar in development to the developed leader. The difference is the perception of the comfort level or style the natural leader demonstrates. We assume someone who appears confident in his or her ability is fully prepared for ownership. This may or may not be the case. For this reason, it is critical to ensure all potential leaders, whether natural or developed, receive the same consistent coaching, evaluation and feedback.

It is in support of this process that the skills of followership exist. Whether a potential leader appears to be natural or developed, the skills to be mastered are the same. In some cases, the natural leader may be at a disadvantage if she or he accomplishes their tasks in a natural manner, because they may never receive the coaching that would help them learn to truly develop their character and to deliver effective coaching to their followers. It is critical, again, to ensure all followers demonstrate the skills necessary for true leadership before bestowing the crest of ownership upon them.

- <u>Overcoming Objections</u>

Allowing ownership is a conscious step leader's take with followers to step them to the next level. Internal ownership is the step each aspiring leader must take at some point. Developing internal ownership is all about taking the step of acceptance and moving forward into new territory. The first obstacle in the process is similar to any selling situation, overcoming objections. In this case, the objections are usually internal objections.

There are many reasons not to take ownership.

- Fear of failure, fear of unemployment, fear of …;

- Loss of place, loss of camaraderie with current associates, loss of …;

- In short, the hindrances are negatively focused around the change to come and the uncertainty of the results of that change. This is a legitimate internal objection. How do you overcome this objection?

There are many reasons to take ownership.

- These are to improve ones self,

- to achieve more,

- to make more money,

- to advance,

- to have a bigger say …;

- In short, there are many reasons to take ownership, and they are positively focused and self-rewarding in nature.

This is a critical internalization of each person's behavior. We perceive certain capabilities and certain ideas we believe we can and cannot accomplish. If our internal visualization is such that we cannot see ourselves performing these tasks, we will fail in that performance. It is kind of like the idea of performing on stage.

When you are working to acquire a stage performance, you must see the performance through the eyes of the individual you are aspiring to portray, not your own eyes. This same process is applicable to ownership of a process or business. If you cannot see yourself as accountable and embrace it, you may have a difficult time accepting ownership.

It is important for the leader to get to know the follower to a depth that the leader can recognize the internal visualization of the follower and coach accordingly. The leader must ensure the follower develops a sound visualization of ownership to both mitigate the fear inherent for some people of ownership, and coach to the expectations of the leader of the depth, style and type of ownership the follower is moving to accept.

In this manner, the internal objections of ownership can be overcome.

**Important Note:** *This is a critical stage in the development of leadership. It is important not to rush the process and not to let the process stagnate. Finding that balance is individual centric, as not all individuals move at the exact same pace. A generic process will rush some people into failure, be slow and cumbersome and bore some people into failure, while supporting most people in the center. However, some of the fast and slow developers will be solid leaders if given the attention necessary.*

The process of working through from worker to leader engages ownership. These steps should be baby steps at first.

*For example, a worker who performs 20 processes an hour only has her own performance to consider. As she moves into a supervisor position, she is responsible for 10 workers, and 200 processes of production per hour. The expectation cannot be that she will automatically understand the supervisor's role, regardless of her involvement in the process. It is different to see someone performing as supervisor and actually perform supervisory duties and have the responsibility for those duties. Instead, the new supervisor's leader should provide coach/mentor services to her on the supervisory processes involved and ensure she successfully completes these with supervision before she is given the ownership of the supervisory position. This will ensure the new supervisor is not dropped into a new role unprepared, which harms both the new supervisor and the production process concerned.*

Moving into any new position or upwards into larger ownership roles, the process should be similar. Nothing is more important to establishing acceptance of the ownership than the relationship between the leader and the follower. If this relationship is built foundationally from day one with mutual support and respect, this development process will move swiftly and effectively and last for the length of the relationship.

These steps must be tailored to the individual and overseen by the leader. This also keeps the leader actively engaged in oversight and development.

Lastly and probably the single biggest obstacle to overcome, and the one that stops many people in their tracks in many situations, is this–acceptance. To own something is to accept it as your own. To own something ties your fate to that which is owned.

That takes courage.

The ritual of development and designation of title gives most people the comfort of having the symbols of ownership and leadership bestowed upon them. This provides most people with the ability to accept ownership as a driver in their development.

However, true acceptance is more than this. True acceptance is an active, conscious embrace of the expectations and reality of ownership.

**Followership Application:**

This is a critical time for you. This is the phase of development where you will either step over the chasm ownership represents, or remain on the safer and therefore limiting side of choice.

To get you across the chasm, you need to build a bridge. The entire purpose of mimicking leader like skills and behaviors through applied followership is to provide you a visualization of the potential leadership offers. It is this potential that supports the structure of the bridge to ownership.

There will be uncertainties and doubts. The courage you must exhibit to your leader is twofold:

• The courage to talk with your leader about your fear, which builds trust with the leader, and

• The courage to face your fear and overcome it, which shows character.

Uncertainty and doubt will stifle your growth. For this reason it is incumbent on you, the follower, to raise these uncertainties and doubts for discussion. If you do not talk about them when they are small, they will grow to become virtually insurmountable. Talking about these issues reduces your uncertainty and stress while enforcing the positive relationship growth you need with your leader.

Many people believe they have courage. However, most people do not truly test this on a very personal level. Facing the fear of failure, and all that implies (loss of position or job, loss of income, family to support, etc.) is a supreme effort. Especially if you just don't try and you can remain safe where you are.

As a follower seeking higher levels of responsibility and career growth, this obstacle must be overcome or you have no future in leadership.

**Leadership application:**

The leaders role in this phase of development is greater than most. This is a critical phase. If the follower does not accept the internal challenge to step across the chasm to ownership, they will be lost. You must be very cognizant of their internalization process. This calls for a significant time investment in coaching.

The strength you have as a leader will be tested in this phase. It will be tested in many ways, but primarily it will be tested through the behavior you exhibit toward your follower as you give them greater responsibility for the performance of their team.

Here we are discussing the real behaviors you must exemplify for your follower to feel a sense of safety and uncertainty. It is a balancing act that only a solid leader can pull off. You have to allow some mistakes, while being especially careful to coach to those mistakes and observant they do not reoccur. This is hard for a lot of people. It takes patience and strength to observe someone learning. But that is, in part, the role needed at this stage.

Your follower needs to learn that you are both a performance driver and coach. Your follower needs to learn that making mistakes do not always or usually cause negative employment decisions to be made quickly. They need that small window of opportunity to reinforce their desire to achieve ownership with the reality of accepting it.

Your follower is going through a tough time. Take time to coach, both on opportunities and strengths. Give the follower some small responsibilities and praise as they are done well. Increase the complexity of the tasks the follower is responsible for to ease them into a new paradigm—owner.

The leadership skill you demonstrate at this time will determine, to a large degree, the success or failure of your follower. This is your responsibility. This is what you own. This is your challenge. This is another opportunity for you to learn and reinforce the leadership skills you possess, as you take on additional responsibility and ownership for a new growth process.

# 7

## *Embracing Accountability*

At this phase in your development process, you are fully experiencing follower-ship as you grow in ownership. The followership you are experiencing is the performance of leadership skill in the absence of complete ownership accountability for that performance. This sounds complicated, but really it is simply that you are at a place in time when you are at the cusp of being held accountable for your performance as a developing leader.

For many people, this is the toughest test yet. But remember, you have been working toward this moment ever since you became the owner of the action of a leader.

In addition to this, you are fully mimicking the behaviors of leadership. The phase of ownership you are in is the assumption of accountability for the processes, operation or people you are assigned. Your goal is full leadership accountability for that ownership. The development of ownership occurs within the context of the demonstration of followership behavior.

For example, let us say there is a conference coming up and the leader usually prepares a business review. The follower, who is learning the skill of leadership and will ultimately become accountable for this review, should be tasked to work with the leader in the preparation of this review.

During this process, the leader works with the follower to explain where the information comes from, the significance of the information, expectations for providing corrective action and plans to improve or means to sustain excellence. The leader takes responsibility for this presentation, but uses the opportunity to coach and train the follower.

The follower must work to learn the process and information the leader provides with the guidance. In addition, the follower should observe the leaders behavior, coaching style and communication ability. Learn these skills so you can repeat them with other employees.

As the follower begins to grasp the necessity of the review, the leader discusses the expectations for completing it independently. As the leader, make clear when that will occur. As in all communications between leader and follower, discuss even the obvious. One of the greatest errors in communication is failing to talk about expectations.

*I experienced this in one team, when I had different expectations than the group when I entered the conversation. It provided a very overwhelming sense of being out of place, out of touch and made me feel and appear unprepared. All of these could have been avoided if my leader and I would have discussed clear expectations.*

This was an eye-opening experience for me. How could I, a very good relationship builder and communicator, be taken aback by something as basic as unshared or unset expectations? As I thought about it, I realized that both my leader and I assumed we each were on the same "sheet of music." It isn't that my leader failed, it is that we were so busy doing the things that needed to be done that we just did not take the time to have a conversation about these basic development expectations.

This is a fundamental flaw with many development processes–there is an assumption that people will be on the same wave length or progressing along a path that is mutually expected. However, many people are just too busy doing the things that need to be done to take the time to level set expectations and development needs.

This is a major focus of this book–the leader and the follower MUST take the time to be supportive, aware and cognizant of the process they are part of. Without this level of commitment and shared awareness, the process will fail.

• Sharing the Load & Transition Management

As with all tasks, once the follower demonstrates the ability to complete this task independently, he moves into a very delicate and tenuous position–being able to share the leaders load.

Sharing the load is an urgent need. Leaders need people who they can rely upon to complete tasks in a timely, competent and thorough manner. Leaders need people they can rely on, depend on, people they know will remain focused and keep the team focused when they are away. Anything less is, truly, unacceptable. As the follower moves into the realm of being an asset to the leader by alleviating part of the workload of the leader, they gain value, both externally from the leader and internally, through intrinsic worth.

*This is a critical time for the follower and the leader. Push too hard and the follower can be limited in their development through the natural act of desiring to please the leader. Not push hard enough and the follower observes the leader pulling back from the commitment to develop and lean more in the direction of using the follower for immediate work at the expense of development.*

Leaders must be careful about this transition. Your followers are learning to effectively follow by imitating your leadership traits. They are learning how to accept responsibility for larger teams and processes. They are learning to think in the bigger picture and evaluate employees working for them. They are learning to coach and develop their followers through observation of your skill in doing the same thing with them.

In essence, followers are usually "whelmed." It is extremely easy for the leader to push too much too fast onto the follower and "over-whelm" them. The feeling of being overwhelmed is an energy nullifier. It does not matter how energetic, positive or motivated you are. When you are placed in a position where the expectations for performance far outweigh the potential you believe yourself to have to complete the tasks necessary to perform, and the time to complete the tasks is limited, you will become both paralyzed and de-energized.

Some people can deal with this better than others, but even in the most prepared person, feeling overwhelmed debilitates excellence. This is an important lesson not only for leaders, but for followers as well. You can overwhelm people in your eagerness to grow them into leadership. Be sure you do not. As a follower, you can overwhelm your self in your own eagerness to be accepted as a leader and acceptance of too much too soon.

The management of this transition time is a critical skill for the leader. You must observe the follower to ascertain their capability to accept more and more accountability. After all, ownership is accountability. Allow the follower the time to experience success in adding new tasks, so they can believe all the tasks can be accomplished and can learn to balance their own workload.

Be careful to add tasks. While someone may appear to be performing their tasks with ease, unless you have spent the time to truly know how they are managing their work, the next task could be the "straw that breaks the camels back." It is, after all, only one task that overwhelms. You must know when the follower is at that point so you do not overwhelm them.

Followers have an obligation as well. Followers must be honest with themselves and their leader. If you are not truly ready to accept the responsibility being handed off by the leader, say so. Otherwise you will accept responsibility for a process and fail to deliver. This will frustrate the leader and yourself and begin a potential path toward failure. Remember the personal characteristics of followership. Live them in all that you do. A leader will respect you for being honest rather than setting both of you up for failure.

Another aspect of this development time is the opportunity for the follower to perform greatly. Accountability accepted too soon often distracts the follower from great performance, because they are too occupied in meeting expectations they perceive as being too hard for their ability. Part of the purpose of practicing leadership traits through followership and assuming ownership in small doses is the chance to experience a positive growth experience.

Nothing provides a boost of energy better then great performance. Taking a team and working with them to improve overall output is a great reward. As an example, let's take the supervisor who has been only responsible for himself and now is responsible for a team of 10. This is a scary experience because of the newness and uncertainty of the position. Enabling the new supervisor the freedom to perform with close support and learn the new responsibility will provide him the chance to see his team succeed.

It is not easy in a business setting to devote the time necessary to develop a follower. Too often, there are so many competing requirements, deadlines and distractions, not to mention staffing and fiscal constraints, that the follower gets indoctrinated under fire.

This is truly the worst experience for the organization. The frontline employees suffer through not having a developed leader to depend on. The mid-level and higher leaders suffer because the business unit the new follower is affecting is not performing as expected. Ultimately the customer suffers because the level and quality of service diminishes as the new follower is brought on line.

Therefore, this time and process of assuming ownership is critical, not just from the follower's perspective, but from the leaders. It is absolutely essential the resources necessary to adequately support this development process be available to accomplish this critical task.

When those resources are in place, the follower is in a position to learn under supervision while tasting the fire to come—but learning effective skills to handle the fire once she becomes accountable for it. This is the critical state. Enable the follower the opportunity to see how greatness in performance is achieved without the accountability for that performance. Let her experience what can be accomplished through effective leadership and the follower will respond positively and grow accordingly.

It is in this manner and at this time the follower will accept and take more responsibility for the followers own development. <u>If they are thrown in the lake to sink or swim, they have no chance to develop success skills. Instead they develop survival skills.</u> When we move them past survival to success we show them it can be done; that they can do it.

A follower who feels this believes this. A follower who believes it will never look back but will continuously strive to find ways to enhance skills and performance, because they are not afraid of failure–rather, they are looking for ways to excel!

As a leader, you need to ensure your followers believe in their ability to succeed. You must provide situations, training, coaching and experiences for them that allow them to experience success. <u>Otherwise, you are giving them mediocrity and expecting them to rise to excellence by themselves. This is an unfair position for anyone.</u>

Providing the foundation of success through situation and example will enable the follower to succeed. It is harder than throwing them into the lake. It takes more effort and a longer time to coach and develop them. However, the choice can come down to take the time to properly develop the follower, or expect to have diminished performance and have to replace the unsuccessful follower in a shorter time than desired.

As the follower, you have an obligation to learn. This requires initiative, which is a great trait all leaders love to see in their followers.

Someone with initiative does not wait for the leader to ask the question, point out the situation, ask for input or ideas, or wait until being told to do something. Someone with initiative is proactive in looking for ways to improve, enhance, correct and change.

As a follower, it is acceptable to take a problem to the leader. However, as a follower with initiative, it is best to take a problem and a solution to the leader. This also demonstrates the beginning of the ownership you are striving to accept as you shift from follower to leader. If you never have solutions to problems, you never demonstrate ownership. An owner would look for problems and solutions.

Self-development requires initiative and ownership of self. You are all you have. If you do not take the initiative to educate yourself and learn what is necessary for success, no one else will. If you do not demonstrate ownership for self-development, you do not demonstrate ownership.

All of these developing skills must be applied by the follower in the pursuit of excellence in performance. The fundamentals are first–ensuring the team or process you have responsibility for is performing well, and becoming the technical expert. Next comes the greater skills of leadership developed through increased accountability through ownership.

As you share the leaders load through your outstanding performance, you discover the greater need to accept responsibility for your own development. You begin to see that true leadership begins within and that this leadership is always awake inside, providing you with energy and focus.

Having this level of commitment to your own development and taking action based upon it, generates a strong desire to continuously improve. Continuous improvement is not just a catch phrase. It is a purposeful and focused behavior.

- Negotiation

There are other process oriented skills to be learned and mastered as well. For example, the art of negotiating is an ownership skill. Negotiation implies a level of concern for the outcome that can only be expressed as something that is felt to be owned.

Someone who only "works here", but does not feel attached at an ownership level, will not negotiate as effectively or be as concerned for the outcome as someone who is operating from a position of ownership.

Negotiation from within ownership intensifies the attention to process, impact, inter-relatedness of issues and true concern for the employees, customers and budget.

It is critical to learn and demonstrate effective negotiation skill. Negotiation skill is not just something to be used for major actions. Negotiation is something you do daily when working with coworkers, followers and leaders to smooth the path towards change and ensure execution is effective.

If you have ever worked with someone who cannot effectively negotiate even the smallest office procedures, you know what I mean. Being able to effectively negotiate is the art of human interaction combined with effective goal setting and achievement.

*I worked with a manager that created friction. The main reason was that this manager could not conduct activity on a give and take basis. Everything had to be rigidly controlled. This is great for a mechanical process, but the people in the office felt they were under siege. She created internal procedures for things as simple as going to the rest room. It was a complete atmosphere based on no trust.*

This type of inflexibility reflects the negative I am discussing. There are normal human interactions that we negotiate between ourselves. If you cannot effectively establish this level of skill in negotiating the daily activities of getting along, how can you be effective in the larger human relationship interaction? If you cannot conduct activities that demonstrate this level of understanding and trust, how can you effectively lead the very people who must actively operate within the process you are accountable for?

There are times when true hard-core negotiations are required. These would be contract negotiations, labor negotiations, and any other negotiation about a contract price or service. This is not the negotiation skill I am referring to. I am referring to the very art of negotiation between people who support processes, between different offices and teams, in order to provide effective execution.

- Evaluation

Effective negotiation skill is entwined with evaluative skill. If you cannot effectively evaluate the situation, how can you effectively negotiate a resolution? And after a successful negotiation, you must evaluate the results to ensure the process is working effectively.

There are several areas of evaluation skill to be mastered. One key aspect of evaluation is developing a fair sense of judgment. Judgment is a characteristic discussed in other places; however, it is a critical skill in relation to effective evaluation.

Closely related to this is competency. As said before, if you are not competent, you will not be fully respected. By the same token, if you are not competent, you do not fully know what to evaluate or have the knowledge to effectively evaluate.

Evaluation skill is a joint skill, encompassing several areas. It is a higher level skill, which is why it is an ownership skill. Owners effectively evaluate their team's performance, and their own effectiveness. Only through constant evaluation can you identify how you should improve in order to achieve and sustain excellence.

Taking this to an even higher ownership level, the owner inspects what they expect. The owner, having established high credentials of competency and knowledge, knows what to look for and looks, often.

It is critical to look beyond the numbers to see the processes, to see the process steps, to observe the inter-relatedness of processes and steps, to see individual people and team performance, to see how training and guidance impact performance, to see how customer impact and attitude affect performance, and to see how each of these areas can be improved.

Inspecting is not a negative skill. Through inspecting, you also find where praise is due. Excellent performance; whether team or individual, must be praised. This is truly what you expect to find–so reward it when you find it through praise.

Additional areas where ownership begins to demonstrate depth of ability is in project and program management. As the follower becomes a true owner of performance, the depth of knowledge and skill of ability grow as well. As these reach their peak, greater responsibility is both sought and bestowed on the owner.

Managing projects and programs takes all the energy you can generate in order to maintain focus, cohesion and purpose for the tasks. This will truly test your skills and provide you the opportunity to demonstrate your ability.

All of these increases in responsibility lead to the final step of embracing accountability. Once this is achieved, the final phase of ownership can begin.

## Followership Application:

This chapter has covered a lot of ground. I hope you see that growth is a very dynamic and changing process. As a follower, you must learn the processes and activities of your business. You must be the expert.

In addition, you must seek out greater responsibility for the chance to have ownership of those processes. Accepting responsibility, which leads to accountability, is your path to demonstrating ownership and continuing your transition toward leadership.

In this phase, there are dangers. As I mentioned above, probably the most dangerous single issue is taking on too much in an effort to please your leader. This can lead to being overwhelmed, and prevent you from achieving your goal.

By the same token, you cannot refuse to take on additional tasks just because you are afraid you may become overwhelmed. If you do this because of fear, you are not being courageous–a necessary prerequisite for success.

This is more about ensuring you have an open dialogue with your leader so the two of you work together to add responsibility in logical, planned steps. This is your major development process. This is the first place where you must demonstrate true ownership and get it right.

**Leadership Application:**

Probably the most critical time is the time your follower is assuming increased responsibility as they move toward ownership. It is very easy to allow them to take on more and more, all the while giving the appearance of being successful, but in reality pushing their life well beyond the limits of balance.

If you do not invest the time necessary to truly understand the development your follower is experiencing, but rely only on how they appear to be doing, you may inadvertently overwhelm them and lose them.

Give your follower responsibility. Let them feel it and understand it. Add additional items in a steady, planned, step by step methodology that gives them time to accept the new responsibility comfortably before an additional task is provided.

If you truly take the time to bring your new follower on line in a solid incremental process, you will have a much greater chance to see them succeed than fail.

No process is perfect. Sometimes people cannot do it. Some people are not cut out to do it. However, given the right circumstances and the leadership of an aware and conscientious leader, most people who have good skill will be able to rise up and succeed. The preponderance or responsibility to ensure this happens is yours.

# 8

# *A Sense of Value and Purpose*

This is the final phase of ownership. This is the place where you step out into a deeper understanding of the role you play and embrace the choices you make.

The structure of behavior you create through mimicking leadership behavior is the very structure upon which you are building your character. The energy you are generating through your attitude of ownership is the energy you must generate to support your followership activity as you mimic leadership traits. As you continue to grow in ownership, you discover the deep inter-relationship between followership, ownership and leadership. You also discover the vast depth of intrinsic value rewards of ownership/leadership.

This is perhaps the single most important aspect of ownerships influence upon the individual. The self-actualizing force created through ownership provides a huge boost to a person's sense of value and purpose, which in turn generates huge amounts of internal energy for self-motivation.

- Choice

We find and measure our value in many different ways. However, we all value self worth and the rewards that come from a job well done. Compensation systems cannot fund this intrinsic value. While compensation plans are important, they do not reach the level of intrinsic reward. Intrinsic rewards are the rewards of choices we make and actions we take.

There is energy in choice. There is an energy generated by a person who makes a choice to behave in the manner of leadership. This energy charges the causation created to enforce that behavior necessary for superior performance. The energy source is ownership. This energy is a huge source of power to sustain development and action to ensure correct and continuous growth into leadership.

The power of choice is at the heart of developing ownership. It is also at the heart of finding value and purpose. It is inherently your choice to move ahead into higher accountability through ownership. It is not that the lack of acceptance of ownership prevents accountability, but that the choice to accept owner-ship and gain the energy through this choice provides you with energy, commitment and drive to ensure that what you are accountable for has a greater chance to succeed.

Someone who only accepts the position but does not embrace the totality of the power of ownership denies the potential for leadership they possess. Instead, they become place fillers and a face in the crowd. However, they do not set them-selves apart as someone who strives to enhance the team and their self.

We have all seen countless people who fit this description: people who have good intentions and want to do a really good job; people who desire the best for themselves and their team; people who always seem to have obstacles in their path, because they do not strive to remove obstacles through choice.

It is a truth that someone who refuses to step into ownership does not find the same level of self worth and purpose as someone who does. How can they?

- Stepping into ownership is a demonstration of perceived self-worth that is rewarded intrinsically.

It is a truth that someone who refuses to step into ownership cannot influence the team as effectively as someone who does. Again, how can they?

- Someone who steps into an ownership role clearly steps into a different level of accountability and action associated with the team's performance.

- <u>Energy & Motivation</u>

All leadership positions require energy. Most require vast amounts of energy. This energy must be self-generated, as there is no external source for the type of energy needed. It is in this simple choice to accept accountability willingly, while demonstrating the characteristics and behaviors of leadership, while under the mentoring of a leader, that true energy is born.

The purpose visualized internally from an energized follower who is moving higher into ownership and leadership is clear. There comes a time when the clar-ity becomes crystal clear. There comes a time when the muddiness in the water begins to settle and you can see your way through. This is the beginning of lead-ership.

The sense of value and purpose then provides a clear path through the chaos to the goal of behavioral leadership skill. This leadership skill enables the individual to grasp the necessity at hand, embrace the choices that must be made, and elevate the performance of the team to a higher, more directed level.

This also provides a huge boost in another area—motivation. All motivation is internal. It is possible to motivate people for a short time externally through fear, high reward or some other out of the ordinary device; but true motivation for all individuals is internal.

As a follower moving into ownership and leadership, self motivation is critical. The energy gained through accepted accountability, coupled with the increased sense of value and purpose, provide a tremendous boost to your internal motivation.

How do you find and harness motivation? First of all, as with any self assessment, you must be totally honest with yourself. You need to ask yourself some questions and be crystal clear in the truth of the answers.

The basic idea is that you must decide and believe in your decision that you are in the place where you need to be and that in order to fully develop your internal capabilities, you must act. It is that simple choice discussed above. It is taking charge of your self and placing your desire on the path of your journey, so your hearts desire and your fear become one. Therein lays the realm of courage.

The difference is that this courage is purely internal.

- You must face your fear of failure and look it in the eye.

- You must evaluate your true potential.

- You must match your true fear with your true potential and make the choice to overcome your fear through your hard work, effort and desire.

- Only then can you truly set yourself apart and truly mine the energy of motivation from deep within.

Once you have this internal motivation energized, there truly is no stopping you from achieving your goal. While there are many indicators of motivation, one that all leaders need to see is initiative. A follower who begins to demonstrate initiative is clearly showing the signs necessary for true leadership.

Initiative is a reflection of ownership. Owners do not wait for someone else to show them or look for things. Owners are constantly observing, digging and finding the positive and the negative. Owners reward positive and coach negative. Owners bring solutions with the issues, rather than just the issue.

Leaders love to have people work for them who demonstrate initiative because it reduces their level of stress. Leaders are constantly engaged and observant, but they need people who they know are behaving at the same level to provide them additional input as to performance.

Demonstrating initiative is a hurdle many aspiring leaders do not achieve. The primary cause of this failure is making that simple choice discussed above. Any choice involves not only a yes or no. A choice also involves energy. One person may say they are accepting the challenge but only mean it half-heartedly. In this case, as soon as the challenges begin to appear they will back off and resume their previous role.

However, a person who says yes with full commitment will see the challenges as opportunities to demonstrate their potential and overcome their fear of failure and raise the energy internally to achieve success. This is true leadership development.

As one gains success through this level of commitment and achievement, self-confidence, internal value and purpose crystallize and the individual continues on this upward spiral.

Do not get me wrong, this is not a path of continuous and only improvement. There will be setbacks, just as there are in all aspects of life. However, the person who is building trust in their internal ability to rise above will find a way to rise above a perceived set back and take charge of their self to reacquire improvement. But a person who does not truly commit will see in a large set back an obstacle that cannot be overcome and will give up.

It is not easy, tapping this internal energy. It takes hard work, chief among which is the ability to truly make the choice to commit everything to a choice. It is looking fear in the face and forging ahead. It is working day after day, hour after hour in a passionate manner to bring your internal belief to light.

- Continuous Growth

As you continue to generate self worth, there are other, more specific or tangible actions that occur. For example, someone experiencing ownership has a desire to know: what are the latest technologies, the latest trends, the newest thoughts, products or processes. In short, the person who owns wants to know as much as they can to enhance their ownership and leadership ability.

One of the ways to gain knowledge is to read. Leadership demands constant information. You are reading this book because you have a desire to know more. An insatiable desire to increase your knowledge is vital to keep your senses sharp and your knowledge current.

It is a good idea to read all of the magazines, publications or literature of your profession. But don't limit yourself to that area.

Read books about leadership, management, the economy, world affairs and other books that help you think, learn and grow. It is important to read books that make you think. It keeps your mind sharp, provides you with additional information and helps you maintain balance. I have included a bibliography of some of the books that I have read, but the list is not complete. There are many other books I have read and there will be many more. My point is to read, voraciously. Learn, continuously.

And speaking of balance—it is a great idea to just read something every now and then for the fun of it. Pick out something you enjoy and just relax while reading. It still keeps your mind sharp, but it helps you relax and decompress.

Another thing that happens when someone feels the sense of value and purpose is a change in self-perception and image. You become more mature and responsible in your actions.

Maturity is not something that happens to anyone overnight. It takes time to mature. Maturity in this sense is a deep understanding of the processes and values of the organization, so your actions support these goals.

Responsibility is closely aligned with maturity in this vein. In this instance, responsibility means being responsible for your organizations resources, processes, people and action. Having a sense of value and purpose brings out a higher level of responsibility.

- Value & Purpose Traits

Your sense of value is two fold. It encompasses the value you feel for the organization and the value you feel for how you are doing what you are doing. Those things we place value in, we cherish and strive to support. There are many items that make up the picture of someone who feels a sense of value and purpose.

- They are more thorough. They have a deep desire to ensure everything is done the right way the first time.

- They maintain control under stress. They know that spewing verbally and emotionally only causes harm to others. These others are the precious human resources needed for success—they protect them.

- They plan. They know that effective planning reduces the likelihood of failure, and enhances the likelihood of above average levels of success.

- They are strategic. They know that the actions taken today must fit in with a longer vision in order to truly enhance long-term performance.

- They implement decisions. They know that effective implementation is the surest way to change the course, set the tone or move beyond the friction of change.

- They promote change. They know that change can be good for improving operations, changing the dynamic, and enhancing overall performance.

- They are competitive. They understand that the business or the operation is always under attack by someone somewhere, and that the only way to achieve a level of long term success is to be competitive.

- They enforce policy. They know that policy is designed for the purpose of improving operations or human relations and understand that abiding by these only helps performance.

- They are actively involved. They know that active involvement is the only way to ensure the processes or business areas they are responsible for get a fair hearing at the table and that leadership is aware of potential pitfalls.

- They are decision makers. They understand that indecision can drain energy. They know that energy is the key ingredient in success.

- They are risk takers. They know that risk taking is a critical skill that ownership drives and leadership demands. Companies only thrive if risks are taken. No risk, no growth.

Transcending ownership into leadership is the simple step of choosing to express your ownership commitment via leadership. As with most things, it's a simple choice. However, the individual skills and traits are far from simple.

Take the last item, risk taker. This is a summary of all the skills and traits we have discussed in this book up to this point. It challenges you to be courageous, it demands you be execution oriented, it requires depth of character, it brings out your best communication ability, it shows how you have developed your internal ownership, it reveals your process knowledge, and it can only be strong if you have a true sense of value and purpose.

All the items we have discussed now come into play. And as we discuss the specific items in this chapter, remember we are constantly adding to our list. There is never a point in time in which anyone masters all the skills simultaneously. True leadership demands constant awareness of your strengths and weaknesses and action to keep your skills as sharp as possible.

By this time, the follower should clearly see the transition being real in daily behavior, attitude and ability. The transformation is one that takes you from an employee with only an idea of a potential change in direction, to a new supervisor learning the basics of supervision and management, up through to a full owner striving for true leadership. The last and final step in this ownership process is one of dynamic impact. As you establish your sense of purpose, you increase your level of commitment to success.

- Depth of Ownership

We are creatures of biology and evolutionary impact. Our genetic background influences, and some would argue, controls our behavior. One of the longest standing realities we have experienced as a species and as individuals is ownership.

As the owner of a property, you derive a sense of value from the ownership of the property and a sense of purpose in the future development and care of that property. You think in terms of inclusion of that property in your daily routine, planning, budgeting; in short, as the owner, you develop an owner sense of purpose that extends beyond the mere fact of owning the property.

Such is the case in ownership of a business, process, team performance and self performance. Owning something gives a sense of purpose. If you have no direction in life, question if you have a sense of ownership over your life. If not, dig in and find out why not.

A leader must have a deep sense of purpose to sustain her through the intensity of leadership. Without a developed sense of purpose, the leader will not have the energy necessary to sustain that performance.

This is the deep ground of the ownership.

As you discover the power of ownership in performance generation, you shift from a position of fearing ownership accountability to embracing it. The main reason for the change from fearing accountability to the embrace of accountability is the evidence of the improved performance you have observed in yourself and your team as you worked through this growth process.

Ownership does not mean being set up for failure. Ownership does not mean you are an island and alone to sink or swim. Ownership means you experience a sense of personal responsibility for your self and others. Ownership means you have a deep understanding of the trust necessary to establish ownership as a true performance background.

Leaders are responsible for creating this sense of trust. Followers cannot embrace ownership without it. If anyone at any time perceives they are being set up for failure, they will fail. If anyone perceives they have no one to turn to for support, they will fail.

If you gather only one thought from this chapter, keep this one: without a sense of value and purpose felt from within, you will not achieve high leadership. You may achieve a leadership position, but not true leadership.

Ownership drives your actions and generates a higher level of energy that will sustain you as you move into the highest level of ownership, leadership. Without it, you are disconnected and only going through the act of leading.

Leadership is the highest form of human capability we possess. Leaders are looked to for support, guidance, direction, discipline, purpose, and a host of other items.

- Leadership requires a fully developed set of values to support the development and demonstration of character.

- Leadership requires a mature and deep sense of value and purpose in order to mine the wells of energy for self motivation.

## Followership Application:

As a follower growing into leadership, the development of your sense of value and purpose is the last most critical item for you to develop, before your true journey within leadership begins. This is the area where only you have the power to step up and do it. Regardless of how much your leader observes you, coaches you of visits with you, if you do not truly "do" it, it is not there.

In this, you must take time to truly discover yourself. This is the truest path to ownership—own yourself. Your leader will give you things to do that will help her evaluate your growth. You must also do things that help yourself to grow.

## Leadership Application:

Yet another critical development phase for your follower is at hand. How well he develops will be, largely, your responsibility.

How can you effectively coach, task, evaluate and observe your follower move through this change in attitude and place? It is a difficult situation to evaluate, and will task all of your leadership skill.

There are things you can do during this time to help your follower shift.

- Ask open ended questions designed to get your follower to talk. Quite simply, at this level, you are pulling them upwards, so most of your coaching should be designed to get them more involved.

- Ask your follower how they think situations should be handled, and why. Again, this pulls them in and up, and provides you an opportunity to evaluate their thought processes, values and commitment.

- Ask your follower what they see as the critical performance or process issues for the team, organization or company as a whole. On what scale are they thinking? If they are still thinking only about their immediate self or team, they have not stepped into a larger context of ownership and an awareness of impact from the external environment.

These are the types of things you must do and ask in order to ensure you provide every possible opportunity for your follower to grow. While it is true the preponderance of responsibility at this stage is theirs, they will not get there if you are not there for them.

The next phase, leadership, is where you need them to be. The current phase—transcending through ownership, is the final building block on the path to get them there. Pour your energy into this phase. Be there for them and set the right example. They need it even while they are focusing internally to find the strength to move into even more responsibility.

# 9

# *Situational Awareness/ Situational Leadership*

Awareness is a key concept in leadership. Awareness digs deep into your situational response ability as well as your strategic and tactical planning/response decisions. Awareness is the active avoidance of tunnel vision.

How many times have you or someone you know been so stuck on a problem or issue that you or they lost sight of the big picture? It happens to all of us. We can become so deeply engrossed in a particular issue we lose our ability to see other things happening around us.

Tunnel vision, or the act of awareness of only one situation, is contrary to the need to develop and sustain situational awareness. Situational awareness is

- the ability to focus on the task,

- be able to clearly see and comprehend the bigger picture occurring around you,

- realize the steps you need to take in each and all developing situations,

- understand the cause and effect of activities, and,

- grasp the ramifications of actions you are contemplating–all in real time.

*Situational awareness is something that I learned as an Air Traffic Controller that has implications in every aspect of work and life, but especially in leadership. As a controller, you must assimilate information in many ways simultaneously. For example, while working the flight data position at one location I had to:*

*1. Talk on the phone with people from different locations or offices passing and receiving various types of control, movement, clearance, flight plan, field condition and other information,*

*2. Listen to the ground and local controllers to mark control strips to keep the movement of air traffic up to date,*

*3. Listen for specific information on departures and arrivals,*

*4. Pass critical emergency information to responding personnel for any emergency situation that arose, and,*

*5. React quickly to all needs at all times.*

*This is multi-tasking at its highest. You cannot focus your attention to one item, because you will miss another equally important item. The requirement was to be situationally aware of everything happening at the same time in choreography of movement. This was truly a symphony of art in motion. Each part had to interact smoothly with every other to keep the process smooth and traffic flowing.*

*As a supervisor, situational awareness became even more important. You were not actually performing any specific task but had to know what each person was doing, if they were being successful, if they were getting tired or about to make a mistake, maintain safety at all times, be aware of weather or field condition changes and have a very heightened sense of awareness.*

Leadership demands this exact skill. As the leader, you must:

- know what everyone is doing without being intrusive of his or her work

- know if someone is operating below potential, at maximum capacity or overload

- know the morale and climate of the culture of the organization and smaller teams

- know the business threats and opportunities, as well as internal strengths and weaknesses.

In short, you must have extensive situational awareness at all times in order to be effective.

Situational awareness implies the leader has an all seeing capacity. Of course, this is impossible. However, the effective leader learns where to look and keeps looking regularly to see changes, trends and any indicators that need urgent attention.

One of the problems many leaders and followers encounter is the inability to adequately see what truly needs to be done because they are so busy doing the things they believe must be done right now. This is a common problem—accomplishing the important task because if you do not do *this* right now *that* may fail.

This type of behavior is action reaction management, better known as "knee-jerk" reaction or "fire-fighting." This is the true fire fighter manager in action: working very hard under immense pressure to put out a fire, but not having any time to build the structures and processes that suppress fires from developing.

In essence, this behavior style is a failure of situational awareness on the part of leadership. Allowing a situation to develop where the leadership team is so focused on "right now" management to the exclusion of providing the resources or planning to ensure right now management is truly ONLY for occasional situations is a failure of awareness. This is a situational awareness issue.

A follower who has risen through the ranks and accepted a promotion to a larger span of control/responsibility position will lose passion and energy for success if he sees this behavior is normal. This is the leading cause of burnout, wherein a person works extremely hard but is not getting anywhere and perceives they will always work too hard to tread in the same position but never move forward. This is an immense psychological issue. It is hard to bring someone back from burnout, unless some serious and sustained process or resource changes are made.

As burnout is a prime driver behind turnover, and turnover is a prime driver to performance, this issue of resource allocation and prioritization is critical. Leaders must therefore ensure they are truly situationally aware.

The changes necessary must be realistic and practical. It does no one any good to have meetings to discuss how to improve the operation on a strategic level if you do not take these active steps and move them down to the tactical level. In this case, a strategy fails.

Rather, look at the true operation as it exists. Do not paint the picture with what you remember what it was like when you held the position years before, or maintain your pre-conceived notions about what it should be like. Instead, listen to what the team is telling you they are experiencing. Make your plans to address the reality of the dynamic you encounter. Ensure your plans address the tactical day to day as well as the strategic long term. Then execute.

This is situational awareness. This is the leadership skill necessary to lead a large organization or a small team:

- Actively being aware of the positives and negatives influencing the team members,

- Actively focusing yours and others energy on effective process modification/development,

- Actively evaluating the business situation,

- Actively aware of threats that change in strength and opportunities that appear and evaporate,

- Actively aware of organizational strengths and how to maintain them, and,

- Actively aware of organizational weaknesses and how to overcome them.

These are situational awareness leadership concerns. Again, situational awareness is the visualization of the entire spectrum of the organizations life. The leader, whether for a small team or a large organization, must be aware of all the indicators and performance characteristics for which she is responsible.

If you are the leader of a small team, you must know each item on each person as well.

- What is influencing your team members?

- How are they motivated?

- Do they have ideas on improving processes or performance?

- Are they performing in a cost effective manner?

- Is there any waste that can be reduced through change?

- Are there any threats to your team's success?

- Are there opportunities for additional business or other activities for your team?

- What are the strengths of the team?

- What are you doing to ensure the team maintains its strength?

- What are their weaknesses and how do you overcome them?

- What are the expectations of the organization leaders?

- What are the business expectations of the shareholders?

- How are changes in the economy, for example rising fuel prices, affecting the team?

All of these questions and more need answering. It is for this reason that situational awareness is not just for the CEO, which it is, but also for all individuals providing any level of leadership.

If you are on top of your game and can answer factually the questions above for your team, your leader will truly respect you and you will gain influence, recognition and ranking. These three are important as you begin to move upward through the organization.

This ability puts you in the picture for a key concept. That concept ties back to a statement at the beginning of this chapter, in which I said no leader could truly know everything about the situation, but learns where to look and looks often. As you are able to provide factual information about the true situation of your team, you may become one of the places where higher leaders go to ascertain the organizations situation.

This is shifting into a high integrity and reliability mode for the leader. Effective situational awareness is based on honesty and factual data, as well as good common sense and correct priorities. Otherwise, your awareness is skewed and you are deceiving yourself.

Leaders learn who is able to generate true information and depend on them for that information. Be one of these.

- Multi-Tasking

As we have discussed, situational awareness involves the ability to multi-task effectively. Effective multi-tasking means only doing as many things at once as you can and maintain your highest level of performance. There is a point at which each person goes beyond the amount that can be done effectively. You must learn this point and remain within your bounds. Otherwise, you become ineffective.

This can be very hard to do as the amount of tasks increase; personnel turnover and you must pick up a task or two until a new person gets up to speed; requirements for reporting increase; and a host of other issues begin to grow. It can become overwhelming quickly.

Being overwhelmed destroys everything a leader is trying to build. If you are overwhelmed, you cannot maintain situational awareness.

- If you do not maintain situational awareness, you miss something that gets the wheel off balance.

- Once the wheel is off balance, you are forced to devote more time and attention to the performance ramifications of the out of balance wheel.

- As you are pulled deeper into the performance issues as they happen, you go further away from the situational awareness position you need in order to balance the wheel.

- The further away from situational awareness you are, the more likely another wheel gets off balance.

- As you try to deal with one situation negatively affecting performance this other one appears.

- As you try to spread yourself to understand this new situation, something else begins to get off balance.

- You finally reach a point where you realize you cannot do all the work, because you are deep inside these tasks and not riding along the crest of situational awareness–your true job.

This is often caused by either not knowing how far you can multi-task, or not developing the skill of multi-tasking as deeply as you need to. This causes you to be overwhelmed, because you are trying too hard to get it all done in a linear fashion, rather than correctly prioritizing and fully utilizing all your available resources.

You have to admit that you cannot do it all. You must prioritize. You must delegate. You must push back to your leader in terms that support situational awareness to keep you capable of delivering performance. Any leader who says not to worry about your situational awareness responsibility, but to go ahead and just get the work done is not a leader to follow, because they do not have either the health of the organization or people in mind.

Contrarily, if you are in a position where you cannot push back, yet you are approaching overload, you must take urgent action to alleviate this situation. This may involve adding additional staff, reducing a portion of your responsibility or a complete overhaul of the organizational structure to better align current or changed responsibility to people.

In any case, situational awareness dictates you know there is a problem and you are taking active steps to ensure the leadership you demonstrate supports the ownership of areas you are responsible for, so the overall organization or team remains highly effective.

- Leadership Style

Situational awareness ties directly into the style of leadership you demonstrate. Each of us has a basic style of leadership. The way we go about executing tasks through people determines our leadership style.

There is a lot of literature on the various styles of leadership. These are generally summarized into three categories: autocratic, participative and free rein. In essence, these are telling people what to do, working with people on what to do, or letting people decide independently what to do.

Each of these styles has appropriate application in the appropriate situation. For example:

- The autocratic style of leadership is appropriate when the requirement dictates urgent response or when the participants are not experienced. In these instances there is either no time to fully explain the reasons behind the urgent action, or the individuals who are required to perform tasks are not highly developed and telling is the most beneficial application. Using this style with a team of highly skilled and self-motivated individuals may de-motivate them and be detrimental to their performance, unless this is a required or accepted process, such as in the Incident Command system.

- The participative style of leadership is generally considered as the most effective style, as it is inclusive of the ability of individuals within the team to express ownership through action. You use this style for a mature team with clear expectations and demonstrated ability. You use this style for most normal activities and operations. However, it will still be required to shift to a different style in case of a situational change in order to maintain high performance.

- The free rein style of leadership is appropriate and available for a highly advanced team of self-motivated performers. A team that is highly skilled, capable and motivated to perform to the highest level can flourish within this environment. Obviously a team that is not demonstrating this level of competency would flounder if left with no guidance or direction.

While each of the various styles has strengths and weaknesses, no one style can provide the totality of leadership necessary for effective activity at all times. For this reason, the best leadership style is situational leadership. In this regard, it is critical to know which style you tend to fall under. It is also critical to create an internal situational awareness that includes the awareness of the appropriate style of leadership for the situations you encounter.

Leadership is about people. For this reason, the style of leadership to select must be targeted to maximize performance from the people so affected. Situational awareness dictates not only awareness of all the factors affecting the organization that exclude people, but most critically the factors, attitudes, behaviors and performance of the humans within the organization.

Having a situational awareness that includes full 360-degree awareness in place and time that is inclusive of all aspects of the organization to include its employees is impossible. However, this is the skill that a leader must constantly be aware of and master in order to gain influence, to inspire, earn trust and be followed.

Situational leadership and situational awareness intertwine into a single behavior through practice. This is not unachievable. This is not just an idea or a concept. This is a behavior that is learned and practiced every moment of every hour of every day. It is practiced until it becomes a standard way of life.

- <u>Other Skills</u>

    There are other skills to be mastered at this level.

- Prioritizes. A situationally aware leader is aware of the many tasks to be completed, some simultaneously, and will continuously prioritize to achieve maximum effectiveness.

- Delegates. A situational leader knows that she cannot do it all. The only way to get all the tasks completed effectively is to delegate to competent staff. This may require developing skills in others so you can delegate to them, but it is a required activity none the less.

- Tough. Situational awareness and leadership demand you be tough. Tough on yourself to maintain your awareness and tough on the processes to keep them under control.

- Observant. You cannot be situationally aware and provide the type of leadership necessary if you are not observant of all that surrounds you, your business, team or organization. You must constantly be living your SWOT (Strengths, Weaknesses, Opportunities, and Threats) analysis as you see change occurring moment by moment.

- Predicting. Situationally aware leaders learn to see the trends and know the performance of their business. They can predict action and are able to predict how their business unit can respond to change. They are looking for change to lead the team into. They are insightful and able.

## Followership Application:

As a follower, you move into situational awareness from the very bottom up. By this, I mean that as a new employee you are able and have the time to learn, absorb and embrace the culture, processes and people of the team. Through this activity, you continuously add new knowledge and awareness of connections, ramifications, priorities and process that impact performance.

It is critical for you to actively engage in developing your awareness. This sounds simple enough, but it takes time and effort. Look at the organizational structure and ask yourself if you know what all the other people or shops on the organizational chart do. Chances are that as a developing leader, you do not.

The greatest tool at your disposal for ensuring situational awareness is through developed relationships. This is a fundamental determination of the breadth of your awareness, because if you have not developed the relationships properly, your team will not provide you with the information you need.

Contrarily, if you have effectively developed relationships with your team as you move into the leadership role, you will have continuous and valid information provided to you that will sustain your situational awareness.

Situational awareness is not just about the people who work for you. However, a large part of your awareness must focus on the environment within which they operate in order for you to ensure that environment is supportive of excellence. Factors you must have full awareness of include, but are not limited to:

- Business Unit Management
  - Fiscal requirements
    - Individual unit cost management
    - Individual unit revenue expectation
    - Forecast and actual
  - Process requirements
    - Work scheduling
    - Training process
      - Technical competence

- • Change management
- • Coordination requirements
- • Threats, Opportunities evaluation
- • Strength maintenance
- • Weakness mitigation
- • Personnel Management
  - • Hiring process
  - • Discipline process
  - • Coaching/feedback process
- • Leadership
  - • Attitude
  - • Relationship building
  - • Motivation
  - • Morale

These are not all the things you must develop a full awareness of by far, but this is a good foundational list to begin your awareness establishment with. The major areas must include the overall business or organizational purpose and requirements, the people within the organization and the leadership application you utilize.

Maintaining situational awareness is more difficult if you do not take the time to establish a comprehensive initial awareness. Without this initial awareness, there will be blind spots in your awareness that will either defeat or deflect you. It is critical therefore, to work with your leader to build a comprehensive checklist of areas you must build an awareness of, which exceeds the area of accountability you have.

Maintaining situational awareness leads to your ability to provide the leadership necessary for the success of your team. Situational leadership is not easy, primarily because this requires conscious determination of the leadership style to be applied, rather than the easier path of responding with your basic leadership style. It is hard to admit that you may not naturally respond to all situations in the appropriate manner. However, this is truth and ground for growth.

Take time to evaluate how you responded to situations with your leader and discuss the ramifications of the leadership style you utilized. Talk about how a different style would have affected the situation. Determine if your reaction was automatic or selective. Based on your discussions, learn to make appropriate leadership selections.

## Leadership Application:

As a leader, you are utilizing situational awareness and applying situational leadership in the development of your followers. You are setting the example they will follow.

If you do not take the time to work with your followers in establishing a clear understanding and active process of situational awareness, they will not understand the importance of the process and will not adapt it as their own. This will only negatively affect you in the end.

However, when you do take the time to do this, your followers will both learn situational awareness and become more successful and beneficial to you. Moreover, they will learn through mimicking your behavior how to coach this critical skill when the time comes for them to teach their followers situational awareness.

The propensity of responsibility for this falls once again, on the shoulders of the leader. That is nothing new.

There are steps you can take to support the development of situational awareness and situational leadership skill in your followers. This is not a comprehensive list, but is a good beginning. You must evaluate your unique situation and determine exactly what should comprise a thorough process for developing your followers.

- Question your followers often about how they see current situations. Ask open ended, non-leading questions, such as, "how do you see (situation) developing?" Follow up with additional questions that provide you with a solid visualization of your follower's awareness boundary. If you do not ask open ended or follow up questions but ask closed questions, you do not have an opportunity to evaluate your follower's awareness.

- Ask your followers to explain their leadership style in a given situation and compare/contrast with other styles. This will cause them to explain whether they made a conscious selection, and provide you with information about their understanding of leadership style selection. This is a good place for discussion of coaching communication.

- Help your followers define the minimum limits of what they need to be aware of. A small team leader obviously does not need to know the fiscal performance of the corporate IT department. Help them form a manageable visualization of what they must know, should know and might want to know.

- Discuss with your followers the expectation you have for their input. Tie this discussion into the situational awareness you expect them to demonstrate. Discuss why it is so important they develop this awareness because of its impact on overall team performance.

Your followers will only become as strong of leaders as you enable them to become. The commitment you make as their leader will directly and proportionally demonstrate to them the importance placed on this subject. As with other commentary in this book, if your process or priority is on "fire fighting," you will have an extremely difficult time truly developing your followers effectively.

Leadership demands placing development of followers in a top priority position. Your followers will know if you make this prioritization through your actions.

# 10

## *Reinforce, Develop, Coach, Mentor*

The behaviors of followership and the behaviors of leadership unite in this chapter. This is simply because at this phase a follower is a leader in every sense of the word, and is therefore demonstrating the same behaviors a leader exhibits.

Leadership behavior is the key ingredient to success in developing leaders. The responsibility to establish hiring practices, create or modify training and development practices and support processes and change the culture and direction of an organization or team lies with the leader.

Leaders must be the first to embrace this process. Leaders must be the first to provide the guidance, vision and energetic support for this process. Otherwise, it will fail.

- Reinforce

A huge role of leadership is reinforcement. What do I mean by reinforce? I mean the very pro-active steps of demonstrating the behaviors you have taught. I mean the very real behavior of expecting your followers to demonstrate a certain level or type of behavior and always, always, always enforcing the standard.

If you do not reinforce the standard expectation but accept what you get, you create a new standard, because you will sink or rise to the level of your expectations. Behave in a way to reinforce low expectations and you will set a low standard that almost anybody can live down to. Behave in a way to reinforce high expectations and you will bring people up to that level.

People tend to relax after they perceive they have proven themselves. The problem with this is the act of relaxation is, in truth, a lowering of standards. Whatever you tolerate becomes the standard. For this reason, leadership demands you only tolerate behavior and performance that exist with high expectations.

Reinforcement, therefore, becomes a tool of necessity for developed teams and individuals. As a leader, you must maintain the high standards you have set at all times. This level of reinforcement of the standard expected ensures the followers and employees sustain their performance to meet that expectation.

There are truly so many things for you to consider needing reinforcement.

- Conversations about character must receive reinforcement through your behavior as a leader and your conversation about the importance of maintaining high character.

- Teaching about the business processes the follower has been growing in responsibility for must be reinforced. You must ensure the importance and energy necessary to ensure the long-term success of the business unit is reinforced.

- Teaching presentation skills must be reinforced through excellent presentation.

- Conversations about trust must be backed up and reinforced by trust.

Reinforcement is the long term concrete of the leadership development process. You demonstrate, teach, observe, coach, demonstrate and coach until the followers behavior is where it needs to be. Then you secure that achievement through your reinforcement of that standard.

Without reinforcement, things settle. The settling process can be that the standard is slightly diminished. If your followers slightly diminish the standard, they will not bring the next group of followers up to your standard, but will only bring them to their new, diminished standard. And then, the next group will settle, resulting in a slightly lowered standard. And so the cycle goes.

It is a critical process. Reinforcement is the only activity that is geared toward sustaining long-term behaviors and performance. All the other activities are designed to elevate, but not sustain.

- <u>Development</u>

It is true there is no substitute for the effective development of followers. Followership demands certain behaviors; however, without the leader providing the example, coaching and explanation, the follower will not know where to go.

Leaders must take the time to develop followership as a standard and expected basis for behavior acceptance for new supervisors and managers. Leaders must set the example and have open, honest communication about expectations with their followers.

- *Remember, a leader without followers is not leading.*

- *A leader with incompetent followers leads a mob.*

- *Only a leader who develops competent followers truly leads.*

It begins with leaders, it thrives on leadership, and it ends with leaders.

- Leaders create the environment where followers can learn the traits and characteristics of leadership and apply those behaviors in their day-to-day activities.

- Leaders provide the environment where these followers can begin to grasp and take ownership of the people, processes or business they are to be responsible for.

- Leaders take these same owners and enable their transcendence to full leadership through effective coaching, counseling and example.

Developing people requires a huge amount of time and energy. In the normal day to day scheme of things, developing people seems to be unimportant, because there are so many issues to be worked on. The business of business keeps you hopping! The intensity of day to day operations in all fields, including the service industry, takes the focus away from individual human development and shifts it to the job.

Yet, effectively developing people is the most important activity, because it has dynamic repercussions on the ability of the organization to perform its requirements in an efficient and effective manner for years to come. It is an investment. The problem with investing is that people tend to not get excited about it because they know it takes a long time to see the return on the investment. <u>But that is exactly the point! If you do not invest in people through effective development methodology, your organization never sees a return and you are continuously fighting the same battles.</u>

The turnover rate today in many businesses is so high it is nearly alarming. People have no allegiance to any particular organization, because they do not perceive an organization as having an allegiance to them. An effective development methodology that truly is focused on creating an environment where development of people is a central tenant of the organization demonstrates an allegiance to the employee.

Take this a step further and you get an organization that is proactively working to get the best out of people and providing the best in return. Why would anyone desire to leave such an organization?

I do not believe they would. Many organizations talk about development, but it is not engrained in the culture. You don't hear very many people discussing behaviors and attitude. You don't see many people focused on enhancing human ability, rather, you see most people focused on reducing the negative aspects of peoples behavior or lack of performance. It is a reverse to what should be in existence.

Leaders must take the time to identify development needs and deliver the resources to meet those needs. Leaders must continuously encourage followers to seek development from educational resources and training opportunities.

You can never go wrong by developing a new skill, either in yourself or your followers. Leadership demands continuous development as a tool for continuous improvement.

- Growth Cycle

Up until this point we have mostly talked about developing the followers personal and business skill. But now it is time to take it to the next level and start to do the very tasks your leader should have been doing with you. Namely, provide the type of relational interaction that enabled you to succeed.

This chapter then, is two-fold. It mixes the discussion of the individual skills and how developing these within yourself is critical to furtherance of your own growth, and the discussion of the application of these skills and development of those you are now responsible for.

This is transitional in nature. In the early chapters we focused on development of personal skill. In the middle chapters we focused on furtherance of these skills and the initial application of these skills to the job. Now, we are taking it full circle and adding the dimension of the growing follower, who is also a new owner, transcending to leadership and beginning the additional task of growing new followers, owners and leaders.

In this respect, the truest development process is revealed. Growth is constant and ever changing. As individuals, we change throughout our life. We gain deeper understanding of life, people, processes and meaning. We do not remain stagnant.

In our development, we go through phases, from being a new worker to an experienced worker, to a supervisor, a manager and finally a leader. We experience different things as we go through these various phases. The experiences further develop us into the next phase person we become.

It is imperative, therefore, for the leader to ensure that the influence on followers as they grow into leaders is positive, practical, accurate, meaningful and proper. These are the very things a leader is striving to accomplish in this chapters discussion.

• Caring

Leaders also focus their time and attention to another critical aspect of an organization or team's health and long term viability. That is the spiritual development of the team. I do not mean the leader becomes a priest and leads the faithful in prayer; but I do mean the leader recognizes the singular necessity to bring the duality of humanity into focus and ensure the spiritual needs of the team are being met.

This is part of the morale of the team. By addressing the intangible needs of the team the leader recognizes the spiritual aspect of the team. Providing reduced cost membership to a local health club, or providing reduced cost day care, or having rooms designated as quiet rooms can all help in this endeavor. There are many ways to recognize and support the spirit. One of the most important is to behave in a manner that demonstrates you care about how you do what you do.

All of these demonstrate the behavior of caring. When people believe you genuinely care about their well-being, they respond in a positive manner. This positive energy supports the spiritual security and spiritual safety needs we all have. Not that people feel their spiritual questions are answered, but that the spiritual nature of the relationships we share is fulfilled.

This is very important. We humans do not exist outside of an energy spectrum. We exist within it. In this book we have talked endlessly about energy. The energy that is generated within each person flows into the people around–after all that is what motivation is trying to accomplish. In this reality is the clear understanding that our existence is dual in the physical environment and the spiritual environment. The joining of these is through energy.

The energy we each create influences those around us. All energy is not accepted as friendly or benign. Some people feel threatened by strong, energy exuding people. As leaders, we must be cognizant of the impact we have on others and show that we care about them, even as we are driving up the energy level consistently to sustain performance.

• Sense of Humor, Tolerance & Persuasion

These next several items culminate in a key skill, coaching. The first item in this is a key ingredient in all aspects of human interaction. It is having a sense of humor. I don't know of many single personality traits that have as much impact as this one.

I have worked for some truly great leaders. I think the one single item I can say about each of them is that they were able to laugh at themselves. That is the foundation of a sense of humor. Everything is not serious. Humor eases tension, it allows people to relax and think.

I have also worked for people in leadership positions who truly had no relationship with humanity. How can you tell? You can tell by their sense of (or lack of a sense of) humor.

I do not mean that people should be funny and laugh all the time. That is not what a sense of humor is. A sense of humor is the ability to not take your self or every situation so seriously that it deters from the ability to still enjoy life. The other thing this does is enable people to still think during adversity.

Leaders who do not have a sense of humor are hard to work for. When everything is serious to the point of life and death decisions even in the most mundane decisions, it takes away the ability to be joyful. Being joyful is a critical element in a successful work environment.

A sense of humor then is both an internal skill that allows you to be relaxed and an external tool you can use to diffuse tension and enable effectiveness in adversity. Even when seriousness is required, a person with a sense of humor behaves differently than one who does not have a sense of humor.

In a serious situation, people understand the need for seriousness, therefore the need to over-emphasize the need is reduced by a person who has a sense of humor. However, for the one who does not, when a truly serious situation arises, they tend to over-emphasize the serious nature and put additional unnecessary stress into the situation. Again, this unnecessary stress reduces effectiveness and creates tension.

Besides, it's just fun working for and with people who have a sense of humor. It makes the time go by faster, generates more meaningful work, and builds the relationships you need for success. People with a sense of humor usually demonstrate the next skill as well–being tolerant. Primarily this is because when you have a sense of humor and don't take every mistake you make so seriously, you can tolerate the differences or mistakes of others.

The sense of humor and tolerance blend together slightly, which results in a true definition of tolerance. Tolerance is the art of allowing people to discover for themselves. That may not sound like a lot, but it is a fundamental skill for leadership. If you behave in a way that demonstrates your low tolerance for people's behaviors, different approaches or learning mistakes, you will not be able to gain the earned respect you need to succeed as a leader.

Everyone does things differently. We learn at different speeds in different ways. Tolerance is allowing people to grow and make mistakes without creating an environment where they perceive that failure to perfect performance immediately is detrimental. It cannot be detrimental to make a mistake.

Understand we are not discussing a specific technical application of a skill. After all, a neurosurgeon cannot make a mistake during the surgery, or there may be catastrophic results. But for most of us, and even neurosurgeons, most activities in life are not that significantly impacting.

The only place you have the opportunity to coach or discipline to modify behavior is when you observe mistakes. Tolerance for mistakes is not meant to be long term, but rather a temporary state or attitude that enables effective coaching. If someone continuously demonstrates an inability to behave or perform, then more serious consequences must occur.

Tolerance is an attitude. Tolerance is the provisioning of a fair and objective attitude towards difference. Difference can be in opinions, race, sex, practices, and ideas; in short, differences are in any area that is different from the person being tolerant. In this case, since everyone else is different than our self, tolerance applies to all people at all times.

Tolerance does not imply that you should allow negative behavior or negative attitudes to run amok or have sway. Tolerance is not a free ticket to enable misbehavior. Tolerance is a temporary suspension of judgment in the interest of furthering the development of the person who is being tolerated.

None of us can be tolerant of continuous poor performance. Nor can we tolerate continuous mistakes or bad decisions. However, it is critical to demonstrate tolerance in the delivery of the leadership process to enable people to feel the freedom to make decisions so you can evaluate them. If you have no tolerance, people may hesitate to make a decision. This stovepipes the process and is a negative reflection on the leader.

Tolerance is a form of oil in the system that prevents friction. A system or process that has minimal friction runs smoother and produces better results than a system or process that is constantly experiencing friction.

Demonstrating tolerance creates a sense of fairness. When people believe they are truly respected and part of the team, it opens them up for persuasion.

Persuasion builds on the above skills, as it takes it directly to the level of interaction with people in order to move them in a direction you desire. If you do not behave in a way that enables you to become a mentor, and if you are not tolerant, it will be difficult for you to persuade others. Persuasion comes from built trust. You do not build trust if you are not high in character and tolerant.

It has been said that leadership is the art of getting things done through others. I agree with this statement, and maintain that persuasion based on positive leadership gets the most done through others.

Persuasion is not as simple as asking someone to do something simple. Persuasion is getting someone to sacrifice in order to achieve success. In order to influence someone and persuade them to support your idea, purpose or direction, you have to have built up trust and personal capital, and understand the art of persuasion. Persuasion is the art of moving people in desired directions with positive energy and excellent results. Communication is the skill necessary to effectively interact with people to persuade.

Additionally, you must now observe your developing followers to ensure their communication is effective. Raising the bar on effective communication, both internally and externally, ensures the entire organizations effectiveness improves as communication skill is enhanced.

- Coaching

The place where you will do most of your personal impact is in coaching. Part of the development of people is the "how you do it" issue. One of the main skills in development is coaching. In this respect it is one of the key skills necessary for leaders. What makes an effective coach? How is coaching different from counseling, and how important is this skill? Let me take these one at a time.

An effective coach is someone who can empathize with the person being coached, to reach them on a personal level. An effective coach brings the best of a person out and inspires the person to perform at that high internal level that demonstrates their potential. An effective coach is engaged in the change and encouragement of the follower.

Coaching is not counseling.

- Counseling is a specific process designed to discuss a specific behavior.

- Coaching is a dynamic process designed to improve, encourage or enhance performance.

As a tool in generating or enhancing performance, coaching is critical. A leader who cannot coach for success cannot raise a team's performance. He cannot inspire or find a deep need within each person to help him or her rise up to the level of his or her internal potential. He cannot even get the person to visualize their potential!

Most of us are not trained on coaching, much less on how to be an effective coach, any more than we are trained on listening. I know we spend years of time as kids in school learning to read and write, yet we spend no time being taught the skill of listening.

We all probably know of coaches. We have seen them in action in one form or another and maybe we marveled at their ability. Or perhaps we never truly saw a coach in action. So what makes a coach?

Part of coaching is listening. Not just for the words someone is saying, but having conversations and listening for the key to turn someone on. What motivates a person? A coach knows, because a coach listens and observes.

While it is true that inspiration comes from a truly inspiring leader, it is also true that the long term benefit of coaching comes from the internal motivation and commitment found within each person you coach.

To reach this level of interaction you must build trust. You must build belief. You must build mutuality of energy, faith, commitment and support. You must create an environment wherein the coached person knows the coach only has her or his best interest at heart and commits all she or he has to rise to the level of performance they are so inspired to achieve.

Coaching also has practical applications to teach skills, discuss strategies and tactics, and define directions. The key to this is that coaching is seeking to find an internal spark to increase into a fire within, whereas counseling is seeking to identify a specific behavior or personal situation and work through to improved behavior.

- Mentoring

The last major item in this discussion is mentoring. The art of mentoring is of itself, worthy of a book. However, for practical purposes, mentoring in this book is limited to providing the adult oversight and friendly discussion of development. Mentoring requires honest and open communication. In this respect, to be a mentor is to be a friend.

Most times the mentor of a person is not the supervisor of the person. Mentors usually are not the ones who have discipline authority over the person being mentored. This is simply because in the mentoring relationship, honesty is necessary. And unfortunately, many people do not feel they can be completely honest with their supervisor.

This is a natural state, really. You inherently know it is wrong to open up about your feelings toward your self, others, situations, etc., with your supervisor. You want your supervisor to see a confident and developing person. This is fair and logical. And it is exactly why having a mentor or mentoring others is critical.

A mentor is considered to be a wise and insightful guide. In life, as in business, there are those who have been around and developed this reputation through their character, leadership, attitude and behavior.

Mentors exist in most organizations, although they are not necessarily prevalent in all. Small businesses may have a difficult time identifying who a true mentor is. However, usually there is someone that you know who you consider to be a mentor.

Leaders who have gained experience over many years shift from the active coach role to the mentor role. Mentors play a unique role in development. The mentor is usually someone who is not necessarily concerned about the day to day performance of the individual being mentored, but about the human development of the person and the macro development of wider knowledge and ability.

All of us need someone we can have an honest moment with. We all need someone we can discuss things with and not have any repercussions. A mentor provides this.

To be a mentor, you must develop the skill of allowing people to be honest with you. You must become the very person you would want to have as a mentor.

I know that some people will say this is too "touchy feely." They would prefer to have a mentor who was tough and directive. But this truly misses the point. Your boss is the one who is more directive and tough. She wants you to grow while performing your job in a manner that keeps her from having to watch over you. That is not mentoring. That is coaching.

Mentoring is providing wise and trusted counseling. You earn the position of mentor; you do not get promoted to it. That is why being a mentor is both a challenge and a reward. It is also why your character and behavior are crucial in order to earn this position.

Mentoring involves listening. I have been fortunate to mentor a very few individuals. I have spent most of the time listening and questioning. Listening enables you to truly hear the undertones of the person. When you have nothing to gain and everything to give, you can truly sit back and listen to the deepest motivations, needs wants and desires of the person you are with.

Listening relaxes the mentoree. They can talk and feel comfortable they had the chance to truly express themselves in a thorough manner. Add to this, questioning for clarity and direction, and you can truly have an enjoyable session in which you can observe the mentoree really think deeply about their progress and growth. It is truly a rewarding experience. It is well worth the effort in building your own character in order to be given this honor.

Your goal as a mentor is to enable the mentoree to grow, while providing insight and ideas. Mentoring does not involve telling anyone what to do. Rather, it is allowing someone to work through the issues internally to arrive at the best solution. This engenders personal ownership and is why mentoring is such a powerful tool.

To be asked to be a mentor is an honor. To effectively mentor is a challenge that will take all that you are to fulfill. Your ethics and character must remain impeccable. Your competence and skill must remain unimpaired. Your ability to think, be self-less and reason must remain strong.

Mentoring is something we all need, and it is something we must all strive to be able to deliver, even if never asked or if never put in the position of being a mentor. The qualities that are associated with being a mentor will serve you well in all aspects of your career and life, since they are a reflection of who you are, doing what you do in your life.

These four major areas, reinforce, develop, coach and mentor, are significant items. Taken as a whole they represent the complete spectrum of your impact as a leader on your followers.

- You continuously reinforce the behaviors you develop.

- You develop the behaviors you need through coaching.

- You coach the skills you need to perform.

- You elevate your personal level of responsibility by becoming a mentor for those you have no personal responsibility for as a means to give back positively.

There is no breakage in this cycle. As new skills and behaviors are coached, they are honed to perfection. As they achieve the standard necessary, reinforcement begins in order to sustain them. As these behaviors and skills are reinforced, others are developed and coached. It is a never ending cycle of energy to move performance to a high standard and sustain it.

Mentoring is icing on the cake for a leader who has demonstrated superior skill in the application of everything we have discussed in this book. It is an honor given. It is a high responsibility.

## Followership Application:

As a follower, you must apply the lessons of leadership to your own development and the development of those you support. You are now looking to find opportunities to reinforce positive behavior and positive performance. You are looking to see where skills need further development for your team and are working to get them that development.

You are also continuing your own growth and looking to maintain your energy at a level that ensures you maintain the standard that you have achieved, while elevating others to the same level.

Followership demands that you continuously work to learn better coaching skill as you continue to coach your team to improvement and success. Read books on coaching skills, attend seminars or classes that provide deeper insight into effective coaching. Always stay in touch with your leader to discuss opportunities for improvement.

## Leadership Application:

This is the tough grinding pattern of continuous, sustained energy. You must keep your energy high as you continuously reinforce the standard and behaviors of success. You must observe and be prepared to interject, as needed, to correct and improve performance.

It is a huge effort of energy to sustain this level and not settle into a lessened routine. But it is worth it in that your team's performance will sustain itself longer and enjoy sustained success.

One danger at this stage for a leader is complacency. If you settle into a routine you think is success oriented, you can allow yourself to be lured into a false sense of success. If this happens, you will not be as observant as you need and by the time you truly see that some things are not where they should be, the deeper rot within will have spread into many areas.

This will mean more and harder work to bring the team back to the level it was. This is wasted effort. If you simply keep yourself sharp, focus on reinforcing the behaviors and knowledge you know to be necessary, be tough on process management, enforce development and continuous improvement in your team, keep abreast of changes in the business environment, economy, technology and other items we have discussed in this book, you will be able to sustain superior performance for an extended period of time.

It is, as all things are, a simple choice. You must choose to get up every day and choose to be focused on reinforcement, development and coaching.

By doing these things, you will, most likely, have the opportunity to mentor. When the opportunity arises, embrace it as an opportunity to finally give back of yourself in the lessons you have learned through actively encouraging and steering the mentoree along the right path of learning and development. Assuring someone else's success is the best reward for your own time and energy you have spent being successful.

# 11

## *Engaged*

Here is a fact that should not come as a big surprise to those who desire to move into a leadership role–<u>you work until the work is done.</u> I have seen a large number of people behave in a less than committed manner while performing in a leadership role. The surprise to me is why they are surprised when they fail.

The time, effort and energy required to develop effective leadership skill is tremendous. The commitment to a team and follow through to ensure their success is tremendous. The energy, time and effort necessary to effectively coach and mentor your individual employees are tremendous.

This is an investment of your life. The return on your investment is your employee's success, your team's success, your organization's success and your personal satisfaction from a job well done.

This is the single biggest cause for leadership failure. You can mouth the words of commitment to leadership, but actions reveal truth. Someone who says they want to be a leader but only works "8–5" is not someone who is committed. Someone who talks about improving their team's performance but finds excuses not to be there when their team needs them is not committed.

This is a very personal choice. This decision to commit fully to this process is all encompassing. The choice made reveals itself through the engagement demonstrated.

Leadership is not a day job. It is a "full engagement lifestyle," that takes a large part of your time and energy. This level of leadership commitment requires a selfless approach to your time and energy. You gain responsibility for development, coaching, discipline, performance and success for a team or organization. Anything less than your all to ensure this success is selling your commitment short and selling those who now depend on you short.

It is for this reason that much is written about the need to find balance. This need only exists because the requirements of leadership are so extensive. It is critical therefore, to discuss this commitment openly with family members so they know what to expect and are prepared to support you in your engagement of this role.

Engagement in leadership does not imply being trapped to a desk. Leadership is not tied to a desk. Managers may be tied to desks, as management is concerned with the specific delivery of processes, revenue, data, etc.; but leaders are concerned with people.

People get the work done. A leader must be out where the people are to inspire, inspect, encourage, observe and provide support as needed. Then the leader must find the time to get all the paperwork complete. It is not and cannot be one or the other. It is both.

A leader demonstrates commitment to the people by the actions she takes in performing the role. This active engagement is personal and active.

This engagement is total. The teams on the loading dock or in the warehouse working the graveyard shift still need to see the leader, even if it is only for a little while every now and then. Stopping by at 5 AM to see them, sit and visit to hear their concerns and needs, maybe bringing coffee and donuts, provides a huge moral lift. This is leadership.

These individuals will believe, not by what you say but by your action of being there engaged with them, when you say you care about their well-being.

Engagement as a leader implies fully participating in all the processes you are part of or responsible for. You cannot delegate your participation in critical processes. You must demonstrate your engagement and participation by being there, fully prepared and ready for discussion, prepared with recommendations as needed, able to talk in depth about the issue under discussion, demonstrating fully your leadership and management skill.

This can be in planning sessions, budget sessions, performance sessions or coaching sessions. In any and all cases, you must be engaged. This does not imply you should not delegate to others.

• Delegate

Delegation is a critical skill that enables you, as a leader, to empower followers and provides you an opportunity to evaluate their performance and ability to perform leadership duties. It is critical to delegate to learn the strengths and weaknesses of followers for more effective coaching and development.

Nevertheless, responsibility and accountability for the delegated action remains with the leader. It is imperative, therefore, not to delegate too much, because you lose the complete awareness you need and your followers become overwhelmed with doing your work to the detriment of their own tasks. Over-delegation is a sign of low engagement in a leader, as they are trying to do as little as possible to get by.

Contrarily, there are times when perceived excessive delegation is beneficial. For example, if you are going to be out of the office for some time and need your followers to pick up your tasks, it may be prudent to delegate many tasks in a fair manner across the board before you depart, to ensure they are capable of accomplishing these tasks effectively. This ensures those tasks are accomplished as needed and does not overwhelm any one person. In any event, this will probably have a negative affect on performance. People can only do so much.

- Time

It is critical to maintain awareness of the quantity of work people are required to perform. To accomplish this, you must be engaged in the day-to-day activities of work.

As talked about earlier, anytime someone is overwhelmed in their work they become ineffective. This is primarily an energy prioritization and utilization issue, and as such is an internal decision process.

Each person only owns one thing in life. We each own our time. Nothing else has the same level of importance to us as our time. We choose how and where to spend it. This choice is the critical issue.

If you look at the 24 hour a day clock, you must divide this up into three major priorities: Personal, sleep and work.

- Personal time is the time you spend with your family or relaxing, exercising or unwinding.

- Sleep time is obviously the time you need as total down time to get good rest and maintain your health.

- Work is the time you spend in some form of work. This can be actively accomplishing work tasks or engagement in thinking about issues and solutions for work problems.

The traditional work scenario suggests 8 hours sleep, 9 hours work (M–F) and 7 hours personal time.

Leadership work engagement demands a different priority. 8 hours of sleep is still acceptable, although some people function quite well on 6 hours sleep while some people need 9 hours. However, for this discussion we will assume 8 hours of sleep. This leaves 16 hours.

The next priority is work. This is flexible, but will often be 10—12 hours a day. Using 12 hours as the average work day, (M–F) that leaves 4 hours personal time.

These are Monday–Friday averages. Leaders also quite often spend time on weekends reviewing performance, evaluating, analyzing and planning.

It does not take too much effort to see the balance shift from equality of work/personal time to unbalanced work/personal time. In a leadership position, however, this cannot be helped. The key is to ensure you enforce certain limits to protect to the maximum extent the reduced personal time available to prevent work from creeping into it.

Take pro-active steps, such as always turning off your cell phone when having dinner, to avoid distractions. This enables you to demonstrate, through action, your commitment to your family and their priority in your life. You cannot exist in a high leadership role if you do not have the support of your primary support structure. You can be a blip on the radar screen, but you will have a very difficult time sustaining your performance. More significantly, why would you want to? After all, success in life is not limited to achieving great work success.

Success in life is the quality of the relationships you establish and the depth of meaning you find in life through those relationships. What relationship is more important than the relationship you have with your immediate support structure?

- You share your deepest emotional attachments with these people.

- You share your fears and joys with these people.

- You share your accomplishments and failures with these people.

- There are no other relationships more important then these people in your life, except for your personal relationship with God.

Engagement in leadership is a heavy burden. There is no doubt or argument in this. But it is not an end unto itself. It must balance with life as a part of life. Bringing in your support structure so they feel they are a part of your success ensures you have reduced stress and support when you need it.

Time at work also requires prioritization. As a leader, you have 12 hours a day in work mode. How much time do your employees invest in work? What do you do with that time? What are the requirements for your employees? What are your priorities? How can you be most effective and efficient in the use of your time?

Time management is an old story and is discussed in a multitude of books. There are organizations that sell day planners and other tools to help you manage your time. Suffice to say that how you do what you do is extremely important. Of equal importance is how you task and evaluate task saturation or efficiency for those who work for you.

*One of the underlying principles of life is that a person can only do so much. As a basic premise, this is indisputable. Human skill and multi-tasking ability can increase the amount of tasks a person can complete in a given time. Technology application can further increase the amount of tasks that a person can complete in a given time. However, regardless of the personal skill or technology, there is a limit to how much a person can do in a given time.*

*Another underlying principle is this—the quality of work produced by a person diminishes in proportion to the number of tasks assigned for completion in a given time at some point. It is finding this balancing point that sustains quality while increasing quantity that is the issue.*

Most people have a full plate at work. Most organizations and teams have worked hard at improving productivity and efficiency to the point that any further improvement may impinge on the quality of the work conducted. In addition, this point, when reached, has a direct and immediate negative impact to the individuals concerned and can lead to deterioration of the work environment.

Here is a fictitious situation in an organization attempting to maximize performance. In this scenario, a person is comfortable conducting 10 tasks a day. These can be management tasks, process tasks or some other reference task. He satisfactorily completes these 10 tasks. His quality is excellent and his attitude is positive. He believes he is doing as much as he should be expected to do and able to accomplish, and is content.

After evaluating this process, reviewing competitor's production efficiency and completing an analysis of the performance, it is decided that this person can increase his task performance by two through improved process management, and by four through improved technology application. The standard this person must perform up to after process and technology training is 16 quality tasks per day.

This increase, while technically doable, is potentially stressful to the person, because his routine will change. He spent a percentage of his time double-checking or reviewing work, which is why his quality was high. As a result, the individual can become more stressed through the higher task performance expectation, and the quality can slightly diminish through modification of process.

Let us assume the quality review checks determine that instead of an actual increase from 10 quality task completions to 16, there are actually only 14 actual quality task completions, even though 16 task completions are attained. To compensate, the task completion number is increased to 18, thereby, it is reasoned, providing 16 quality task completions.

However, as the number of task completions is increased, the quality again diminishes. Now 18 tasks are completed, but only 15 are quality task completions. The individuals performing the tasks are much more stressed and the entire system is beginning to grind with friction. Not to mention the increased cost from waste.

Still, in order to meet the "proven" goal of 16, the number of tasks is increased to 20. However, because of increased stress and tension within the individual completing the tasks, only 15 quality tasks are still completed. In this instance, the workload has doubled but the quality performance has only increased by half, and waste is still increasing, which equates to even higher cost.

In this case, the individual within the process is becoming too stressed to perform at his peak. In this case, he will begin looking for other work to do because the stress involved in this performance expectation matrix is too high.

This is where a follower and leader must be engaged. A follower/leader would observe the ramifications of the changed performance expectations on the employees and provide feedback. A follower with courage would tell it like it is and let the leader know this expectation is too high and provide an alternative solution. A leader with courage would also raise the concern, because their situational awareness tells them that not only are they facing an immediate quality task completion problem, but they can see the further ramifications of the increased stress on the team and the increasing costs. The visionary can see higher turnover and knows now is the time to act to prevent this scenario from developing.

The engaged follower/leader will be able to provide higher leadership quick input, recommended solutions and realistic expectations based on the reality they see. However, if the follower/leader is not engaged but is only there for the day job, they will not see the wider implications. These types of follower/leaders will wonder why their process is failing, blame any issues on upper management, and will not see the failure coming until it hits them.

*In-flight collisions occur (very rarely) because the pilots did not see each other. Pilots do not see each other for many reasons, but here are two. First, they are not fully engaged in constantly scanning the environment for potential aircraft, and two, because the plane that is going to hit you is not moving across your field of vision, but is growing in size very slowly in a rather stationary point in space.*

Leadership engagement is very similar. You must scan through your situational awareness constantly; be a visionary who can understand and see potential situations; and be fully engaged in the whole range of potential ramifications and actions, and how they affect your team, self and organization.

Nothing less than full engagement is acceptable in a leader. Anything less than full engagement is an accident waiting to happen, and in most cases harm much more than just the individual leader who is not truly engaged.

There are several other areas in which the engaged follower/leader must excel.

- Defines needs. True engagement means you are aware of the needs within your team. Further, as a fully engaged leader, you can define and clarify the needs within the team and organization in terms of tangible and intangible needs.

- Analyzing. Engagement means you constantly and continuously analyze data. You are constantly looking for trends, patterns or anomalies in performance that will give you the earliest possible hint that a process is out of control or a team is in need of help.

- Facilitating. Engagement demands a high level of facilitation. This drives from the full awareness of people, processes, change, technology and other factors that cause people to need recalibration and skill/process re-tooling. Being effective in facilitation reduces the friction associated with change management and expedites movement toward sustained success.

- Defines Evaluation Strategy. Engagement requires a depth on understanding that elevates the awareness of strategic value in how and what we evaluate.

- Manages Organizations. Engaged people manage a lot. They manage processes, budgets and organizations.

- Sets Goals. Engagement means a mature ability to constantly evaluate and set goals that are challenging but doable, and constantly being aware of performance in relation to goals.

## Followership Application:

Full engagement of your skill, energy, attitude and awareness marks the last step in your individual journey to leadership. This is the full application phase of leadership. At this time, you:

- are fully developed as a communicator,

- have exemplified character,

- can effectively execute all your assigned tasks,

- have the developed confidence to be courageous in coordination and communication,

- actively demonstrate internal ownership,

- feel a true sense of value and purpose in all that you do,

- practice and experience active situational awareness,

- consciously apply situational leadership,

- see the overall picture from a position of visionary, and,

- bring all your senses and talents to the table as an actively engaged leader.

In short, you have arrived at the final threshold of performance leadership.

Engagement is hard and fulfilling. It means taking doubt and setting it aside. It means being selfless in support of team needs. It means digging deep for the energy you need to truly step up to the expectation of leadership and delivering a home run.

It also means success in your transformation from worker through followership and ownership to leadership. Being empowered to actively engage implies true team participation. You are a member of the larger team at this time and have impact and influence in the larger team arena.

If you doubt that you are fully engaged, you raise the question of doubt in your mind. At this stage, you should have no doubt. At the same time, you should have regular conversations with your mentor/leader to validate your direction, purpose and place within the team.

There are no further steps to develop leadership except continued gained experience and assimilation of that knowledge and experience. The next step for you will be to begin the process of developing your followers, which will provide new perspective and learning for you as well.

## Leadership Application:

Congratulations! You have successfully coached an individual to being a new leader. At this time, they are fully engaged and committed to the success of the team. At this time, they will begin to take ownership to develop their own followers, having your coaching as their example.

This is not the time to reduce your engagement with your follower. This is a time when their active and full engagement will require your support more than ever. They will need reinforcement and oversight. They will need your ear to discuss issues and situations. They will need your knowledge and wisdom.

It will require even greater situational awareness from you to watch over their new confidence. They are eagles soaring on high. They have the strength and energy of a giant. They have not yet, however, learned the lessons only age and experience can teach. For this reason, even if they do not say it or show it, they need you.

You must remain engaged with these new leaders as they begin the process of raising a new generation of leaders. You must ensure the process is followed effectively and the development is fully completed.

While this is a time of celebration, it is also a time to watch and coach. Remain engaged.

# 12

# *Visionary*

What is a visionary? Why is the skill of visioning important in a leader? The answer, while quite simple, has huge ramifications for teams and organizations. The answer can be demonstrated in the following. A new employee asks the receptionist which direction he should take. The receptionist asks the employee where he is going. The employee says he is not sure. The receptionist then says that it truly does not matter which direction he chooses to go.

- A leader that has no vision will lead an organization to that end.

- An organization that does not know where it wishes to go will get there.

The problem in both of these statements is that the destination achieved probably will not be exactly where it should be. Nevertheless, even if no one provides a vision, the organization will still go somewhere.

Vision is the leadership skill of seeing the potential of the organization or team and enabling the organization or team to meet or exceed that potential. A visionary sees not only the potential for excellence, but also the potential for failure. The visionary provides the guidance necessary to overcome potential failure to reach potential excellence. Visionaries do this because they have achieved excellent situational awareness, and because they connect to life and the life of their team or organization.

Life is change. Organizations are made of humans who experience change. Processes and products change. The weather changes; in short, everything changes. This is a constant reality.

The point of vision is to take natural change energy and focus it into a desired direction so the energy of change is focused and directed, not random or chaotic. Leaders inherently must know how change is affecting the organization, where the organization is and where it must go.

The visionary is the leader who is eyes wide open. The visionary is constantly looking to see reality and provide a clear path to achieve the vision of the team.

- A visionary sees threats, and takes active steps to prepare for them.

- A visionary sees opportunities and engages the team to take advantage of them.

- A visionary sees weaknesses and develops strategies to overcome them.

- A visionary sees strengths and maximizes them.

Competition has no time for organizations that do not see threats. If you are not aware of threats and take no action to prepare to meet or overcome them, they will overwhelm you to your failure.

Business today competes not just with the business next door, but also with businesses around the world. Information technology and transportation have reduced the area of "competition safe," from a region within a country to near nothing. Today, there is no competition safe area.

Visionaries understand the organizations weaknesses. A leader constantly evaluates and analyzes the organization to identify weakness. A leader creates energy and directs resources to counter weakness to create strength. Weakness is most often overcome through long-term strategic planning and effective execution of those plans.

Weaknesses also are overcome through targeted hiring of specific individuals with necessary skills to quickly overcome a weakness. In any case, the leader must create, support and sustain process to constantly evaluate and overcome organization weakness.

Visionaries always know their team's strengths. Visionaries are constantly aware of the need to constantly review and evaluate strengths and provide process to support and sustain them.

An organization's strength can shift as the people in the organization shift. It is critical, therefore, for the leader to be constantly on guard to sustain a balance between the needs of the organization for effective performance, and the strengths of the organization and its ability to meet those requirements.

- Vision Statement

Many organizations create vision statements. A vision statement is not the same as a visionary leader. At the same time, visionary leaders must create vision statements that reach everyone in the organization and bind them to a path or direction.

The visionary leader knows that the people of an organization are the ones who execute and live the vision. By creating a vision statement that inspires and directs the energy of the team onto a similar path, the leader supports the creation of organizational synergy. This in turn creates a purpose and strategy.

The vision statement is not just something that you hang on a wall and tell everyone to memorize. Instead, the vision statement states the organizations core purpose. <u>It provides the fulcrum from which to leverage direction and purpose.</u> It provides a unification point from which all changes in the organization flow to strive for a purposeful accomplishment.

*A vision statement provides the basic premise for organizational structure. In essence, it is the executable purpose of the structure.*

If the organization has a vision that provides this structure, the leaders of the organization have the capacity to fulfill the steps needed to effectively lead.

Even when a vision statement is completed and is the most beautiful, inspiring, perfect statement imaginable, it still takes visionary leaders to live it. Leaders provide the energy and belief behind the vision. To provide this vision you must use all the skills at your disposal.

Visionaries must demonstrate outstanding people skill. Visionaries understand that everything they do must support an internal vision of dynamic positive change. Change is a people issue, because change impacts people. Processes and technology are changed, but do not experience emotional change. This emotional change is the critical issue for visionary leaders. Effectively move an organization through change and greatness results. Ineffective change movement leads to reduced results.

A visionary leader creates teams of people who are truly demonstrating followership, ownership and leadership. A visionary leader inspires these teams with purpose and lofty goals, while ensuring the day to day activities of business are completed in the most efficient and effective manner possible.

• <u>Share The Credit/Take The Blame</u>

How many times have you achieved something and heard someone else take credit for it? How many times have you, as an active member of a team, heard someone take credit for the team's success?

Have you ever watched someone when you know they did a great job at something, you know they expected some recognition for their performance, hear someone else take or get credit for it? It is a visible deflating experience.

*I remember when a friend of mine had completed a tough business project. The results of his effort were excellent and provided the business unit with a very comprehensive analysis and proposal for improvement. When we were all brought together for a meeting, I assumed he would get recognized for his effort, and so did he. So when our boss was talking about this project, I was watching him to see the energy that goes with the individual pride in a job well done.*

*You could literally see him deflate as our boss spoke about how he had completed this analysis and how he had provided a direction for the team, etc. He never even mentioned my friend's name. Everyone else knew the truth as well, so the entire team took a backward step. And there simply was no reason for it.*

Leadership demands you share the credit and take the blame. Nothing else truly works. You must not hog the glory as the leader. After all, the very people who are deserving of recognition are your followers, and it only makes your entire team perform better and look better when they perform well. By taking the recognition away from them you only harm yourself through poor motivation of your team members.

As a leader, you need to seek out opportunities to provide recognition. Most people only recognize poor performance. While it is necessary to identify and correct poor performance, this does not generate positive motivation. Recognition of excellent performance, however, is a pure positive experience and supports employee motivation.

The actions you take as a leader reinforce the culture and environment you seek to create to achieve the maximum performance from your team. By sharing credit with others, you reinforce the positive nature of performance and the culture of fairness you need to keep your team motivated.

Visionaries understand these principles and apply them at all times. A visionary understands their role is 24/7–they cannot be less than their role requires.

Visionary leaders share other similarities as well.

- A visionary is trusting. She knows that broken trust is a catastrophe waiting to happen, because it will create poison that will destroy the team.

- A visionary influences. Influence is the major strength of long term effective change. While a leader can direct change, a visionary influences others in a way that enables them to imagine, embrace and live the change in a more effective and long lasting manner.

- A visionary speaks. Public speaking, whether to stockholders, employees or the public, is critical for a visionary. You must understand how all the various constituencies will interpret your remarks and phrase them in a way that all can embrace. This sounds a lot like being a politician, and it is. A visionary for a team cannot isolate a constituency, because he knows that all of them are important for overall success.

- A visionary is sociable. A visionary understands the need to be on that loading dock to see the night shift. He understands that his physical presence is necessary as a tool to show his concern and engagement with the team. He knows that by being there, he can provide positive energy to support all the team members in the path to success.

The position of visionary is the pinnacle of excellence, achievement and recognition for a leader. This is a place that is at the very tip of the spear in terms of change management, energy generation, value enforcement and a host of other items critical for team and organizational success.

It is extremely important to understand that the ability to implement the skill of visionary is the culmination of all the learning it takes to be an effective leader. A true visionary lives the role constantly.

As a leader who is not the CEO of the organization (which includes the vast majority of us), visioning is a critical skill to master as well. The ability to grasp the designated leader's vision and mesh your team vision with the larger vision is also a step into being a visionary.

As a person who does not lead a team, understanding the necessity of having a vision of life and the capabilities that exist is a step into being a visionary on a personal level. It also implies success in self discovery and self leadership–where all true success generates.

There is no higher attainment for a leader than to achieve the level of visionary. It takes mastery of everything we have discussed in this book. And that is no short order. It takes dedication, commitment, self-sacrifice and hard effort to achieve this level of leadership. But it is worth it.

## Followership Application:

For a follower, the best thing to do in the search for vision is to be close to, listen to and speak with the visionary in your organization. Who is setting the tone? Who is driving the team? Who sets the direction? That is the person to visit.

When you visit, don't just sit and listen. Ask questions. Ask why a certain path has been chosen. Ask what the greatest challenges are that the visionary sees. Ask what the opportunities are that the visionary sees. Think about some questions and always have at least two that are valid and demonstrate you have taken some time to think about this encounter.

When you do this, you show your commitment and engagement. These are your leadership traits rising to the surface. This is the type of thinking that will one day lift you to the status of visionary, as you learn how a visionary thinks.

## Leadership Application:

Being a visionary is difficult, even for someone who has mastered the skills of leadership. Visioning is the natural progression of thought for the leader, because you fully understand the value of looking to the future to establish a place you can pull the team towards as you guide them in the present.

Being a visionary is the most important skill you will master as leader. You have to master the art of providing effective business successful employee supporting pathways through the chaos towards a place that all can visualize as the place they should be. It is not easy.

This will be the final hurdle to higher leadership skill. This will be the one that will test your resolve, your energy and all your skills. However, when you provide the right vision in the right way and the team responds and chaos is leveled and success is attained and sustained, the rewards are beyond any that can be measured.

# 13

## *General Discussion Topics*

There are many situations that do not neatly fall into the general development categories we have discussed. For that reason, I have added some specific conversations about some specific items you need to consider and think about. Everything that a follower and a leader do has ramifications. This chapter discusses some potential ramifications or situations to spur your thought process. These are not the only solutions to these topics, but ideas to think about, talk about and review as you grow and establish/evaluate your processes.

1. Compensation Implications: Taking an individual from their current performance level and raising them to a higher level will have compensation implications. As a fundamental summary of the compensation process, remember that a compensation system must be perceived as fair to the individuals within the system, or it is ineffective.

If you take an individual who is currently working as an individual performance unit and promote that person to a position where she has 10 people to supervise/support, there are compensation implications. As this person improves their supervisory ability, there are compensation implications.

Additionally, as this person moves from complete inexperience in this position to a higher position of learned and demonstrated followership and leadership skill, there are implications. As the individual moves into a deep ownership experience and transcends into a true leader, there are implications.

Most compensation systems address a base line wage that ties to scales developed through wage analysis. These programs provide a very good reference point for wage discussion. However, to lock individuals into a system whereby they receive only a certain wage based on factors like time with organization or span of control does not compensate the individual for their internalized sense of value, or necessarily the value they bring to the team.

In other words, compensation factors that do not reflect the value for the company the individual possesses through their increased development and ability do not necessarily provide the compensation the individual needs to maintain that energy level and performance edge.

It may be necessary to work with individuals to ascertain how they perceive compensation and mutually recommend changes to the structure that fit the needs and aspirations of the individual, while ensuring costs tie to sustained or increased performance delivery. This type of compensation model would further support ownership philosophy and further tie the individual to the organizations success, while providing the individual with both intrinsic and practical recognition of their performance.

The rigidity of many organizations, when it comes to who can be paid what, stifle this type of individual recognition. They should not, but they can.

2. Doubt: Doubt is primarily a destructive element. A seed of doubt can eliminate all the positive energy you have. A performer who has multiple decisions questioned begins to doubt their ability to make effective decisions. A sales team with doubt in their ability will live down to their belief.

Doubt is insidious. The source of doubt is usually not something that is easily identifiable. However, it is critical for the follower and leader to develop a keen sense that enables recognition of this phenomenon. With this sense comes a need to learn all the factors possible that can impact your team and generate doubt.

Sometimes, it can be as simple as an increase in the performance requirement that brings forth doubt. After all, if you are already busting chops to deliver the current performance requirement and then it is raised, it is very possible to doubt your ability to further increase productivity.

As leaders, it is critical to evaluate the impact of decisions on the psyche of the individuals who will have to execute these decisions, to ensure you do not increase doubt.

Once doubt is in place, it is very difficult to eliminate. It takes a true level of empathy, positive motivation and refocusing of the team's perspective to remove doubt. While this can be accomplished, it is a needless exercise that should be avoided, if at all possible.

3. Initial Assessment and Development: As a new individual is promoted into a new position, there are assessment, capability and development issues that must be addressed. The best process is to have exactly that in place–a process.

The appearance of organized process, especially in the midst of upheaval and newness on the part of the new employee, provides a sense of surety and certainness. This leads to a feeling of acceptance and trust in the guidance of the leader and enables the new employee to focus on the items you know to be critical for success. Establishing this trust is a crucial first step.

In addition, you must ensure there is 100% knowledge passed and 100% task coverage. This requires documentation of the training and development process. Take a look at Chapter 14, Initial Assessment and Development of New Employee. Use this as a foundation to create the specific, targeted process you envision as the one that will lead to 100% success.

It cannot be over-emphasized that the initial exposure, just like first impression, cannot be accomplished a second time. You only get one shot at this. Use all the resources at your disposal to create, support, target, drive, evaluate and ensure your employee development process is the right one for each employee.

4. Delivering Feedback: Feedback is a consistent, constant and dynamic process. Feedback occurs at all times. There is no time when feedback does not occur. Even not giving feedback to someone is construed as a type of feedback. For example, if someone does something that is less than acceptable performance and the only feedback they get is their supervisor ignoring it with no real coaching or counseling, they will assume (makes an ASS out of U and ME) that their behavior was ok.

The key then is to ensure you deliver feedback that is appropriate for each and every situation where feedback can take place. And as feedback takes place at all times through formal, informal, verbal and non-verbal means, the ultimate key is to be aware of the feedback you are providing.

In this, awareness of presence is critical. This feedback ties in with situational awareness. You must be aware of who is around you, who can see you, who can hear you, who will read what you write, etc. You must be diplomatically focused so you provide the correct spin on what you say by being honest and thoughtful before communicating.

This is not an easy task. Quite the contrary, this critical and hard-learned skill takes much effort to master. The rewards are exceptional for your self and for those you affect. The ability to positively influence morale and the energy of the team ensures higher success and improved or sustained performance.

A major activity of delivering feedback is delivering disciplinary action. The purpose of discipline is behavior modification. Discipline is not setting people up for failure and firing. If this is the reason you are using discipline, then you are failing the individual concerned.

Discipline hopes to find a source or connection with the person receiving the discipline in the expectation they will learn from the discussion, change the negative behavior, and turn it into a positive behavior. Anything less than this is unacceptable in the disciplinary process.

It is critical to have this conversation with the person being disciplined. He or she must understand deeply that the true goal of the process is to help change behavior so she or he can perform in a way as to make them a viable part of the team. In order to accomplish this, you must truly believe it and desire this result. Otherwise, your body language and overall communication will reflect the truth that you are not being pro-employee, but just filling the blanks on the way to their termination of employment.

New supervisors and managers should attend formal training on the proper way to deliver feedback. This is a complex and extremely important aspect of becoming a leader. Leaders must demonstrate this behavior in all interactions so the followers see and can emulate this behavior.

5. Education: Education is necessary in the career environment. To be truly effective as a follower, and especially a leader role, you need education. There are two types of education and both have validity.

First, there is the education you get through living. I have met many people who have not completed a "full" education, but who have the smarts and savvy to succeed. They have not sat back and just let life go by. Instead, they are astute observers of the human condition and have developed their skills to match the knowledge they have gained. These learned skills are equally as important, at times even more important, than any formal education.

The second type of education, of course, is formal education. There are many classes people should take:

- If you hope to spread ideas, convince others of your positions, explain issues in depth or a host of other reasons, you must learn how to write. For this reason, taking grammar or writing classes is a very good and useful idea.

- To gain a deeper insight into the workings of the motivations of the people around you, it is a good idea to take some psychology classes. Not anything in particular and not to a degree level, but a few basic psychology classes provides a sound basis for establishing and enhancing your understanding of human development.

- If you are in the business environment, you must complete business classes. To have a true understanding of the processes, financial strategies, performance ramifications and business environment, you need to take those classes which educate you to the business environment.

- If you are in the service environment, you should take classes that provide enlightenment of service processes. Providing services is no less demanding than performing in the business environment and education can provide you an edge to achieve excellence.

All of these are good ideas, however, remember it is up to you to take the initiative to complete your education. You are the individual responsible for your development—no one else is. You are the one who must seek out opportunities to learn—no one else will. You are the one who will ultimately determine your accomplishments—no one else will.

6. Goals: A key skill for all followers and leaders is the skill of setting good effective goals. It is a skill that will support your entire career life. Setting goals requires the ability to balance priorities, an active and developed situational awareness, a keen intuition, and the flexibility to roll with change.

Setting goals must be based on reality. Goals that are not reality based are destined to fail. Additionally, ineffective goals lend themselves to the creation of doubt and the generation of negative expectations. Both of these must be avoided at all costs.

Effective goals marginalize false hopes by bringing reality into the process. Effective goals marginalize unrealistic desires to achieve higher or further than can reasonably be expected. Effective goal setting ensures you personally, and your team and your organization create paths for success that are genuinely challenging, but genuinely doable. Effective goal setting is a catalyst to successful performance. With it you can achieve many things, without it you will work much harder to go half as far.

7. Spirituality: Spirituality is a vital internal process for everyone. The work environment should not become a haven for spiritual growth and development; however, it cannot be a place where spiritual potential or values are blatantly over looked.

All the processes involving people must be viewed not only in the manner of ensuring business efficiency and effectiveness, but also in the manner in which they support the spiritual balance people need to feel they are being treated fairly, or that the processes are established to support fairness.

Fairness does not imply easiness or haphazard implementation. Fairness means that the individuals can understand the necessity for the process, that the process is possible to complete through effort–achievable, and that the ramifications from failure match the needs of success.

Spirituality does not mean creating temples to worship. Spirituality means delivering work needs in a way that supports human capacity for change, effort, achievement and work. Fairness is one aspect of spirituality in action. Another is how we communicate what we need to communicate.

When you overlook the spirit of your employees, you miss the opportunity to build a team that can sustain great performance. Spiritual energy is a huge resource, that when tapped properly, yields solid benefits. This is probably the hardest to achieve in today's business environment, when so much is focused on the bottom line and human cost, rather than building true human potential.

8. Personal Success: It is important to define what success means to you. What is success? Is it a higher paycheck? Is it only if you become the CEO? Is it surviving in a cut-throat environment?

Success is defined differently for each of us. The problem is that if you do not know what it will take to make you feel successful, you can work very hard for a lot of years and always end up feeling second fiddle.

Success, to me, is the knowledge that I achieved every task given to me with excellence. I am successful. Success is an attitude and a way of life. There is no magic location in the future that will suddenly enable me to feel success. Success must be something that is felt in the only time that matters–now.

If you do not clarify or quantify what you believe your personal success to be, you miss out on the opportunity to deliver it. Have you ever led a team and had no goals? I have. And it is a self-defeating leadership role. Anyone who does not know what they must do to achieve success cannot be successful. For that reason, on the occasion of being given a team, I always quantified goals to give a sense of unity to the team as we moved forward toward success.

This is the same process and energy necessary for internal motivation. Take the time to visualize what success means to you. View it through your sense of values and purpose. Talk about it with someone you trust. Figure it out. Become it. Be the success you believe you need to be to be successful. Then you will always be successful.

This is a tremendous energy generator for your self as you face unpredictable team performance and the constant change in the business environment. If you believe you are a failure because you have not identified or achieved some unknown "success" model, you become debilitated and unproductive. But if you feel that how you do what you do defines success, you can take the team through the challenges of performance and the business environment and come out with a demonstrated successful team performance.

9. Giving Back More Than You Get: Altruism is not something that only exists for those who are wealthy. Altruism is a noun that is the principle or practice of unselfish concern for or devotion to the welfare of others, as opposed to egoism, which is the habit of valuing everything only in reference to one's personal interest; i.e., selfishness.

Altruism is also not to be confused with philanthropy, which is altruistic concern for human welfare and advancement, usually manifested by donations of money, property, or work to needy persons, by endowment of institutions of learning and hospitals, and by generosity to other socially useful purposes.

Altruism is simply selflessness. Why would this attitude of selflessness be important? Because it supports value and generates energy within to utilize in team motivation and self motivation.

There are few things that will make a person feel good more than doing things for others because it is the right thing to do. This type of intrinsic feeling firmly brings your spiritual nature in line with your physical reality and enables a higher level of successful living than any thing else.

10. Learning Followership as True Leadership: It shouldn't seem odd to start a journey following someone who has experience with the path you are walking. It is logical.

The person ahead of you knows where to step for safe footing, so you step the same way. The person ahead of you knows when to stop and look, so you stop and look as well.

Essentially, this is the follower mimicking the leader. That is the basis for learning effective leadership skill. As you mimic the leader's behaviors, you learn them. As you learn them, you become experienced in them and before long, you are on the path with no one in front, but with someone behind you, watching where you step.

11. Email etiquette: Few things are as useful in the new modern technological world as email. They give you the opportunity to share the same information with multiple people simultaneously and send massive quantities of data. They are just plain useful.

They are also one of the most irritating communication tools. Why, because what is not said in an email is the full spectrum of information surrounding the communication. What is missing is:

• Intent

• Purpose

• Emotional attachment

• Voice

• Tone

In short, all of the things we normally receive from people when we communicate with them are missing. This is not a problem except for one thing–people imprint into the email the tone they perceive you are using.

This can be disastrous for effective communication. So truly think about how what you are writing will be interpreted before you send it out. Only use email for information or data–call someone on the phone if it involves anything else. Set people's expectations about the use of this communication tool, so the negatives can be avoided. And always be aware that no matter what you do, someone somewhere will interpret your words in a way that you did not intend and you will have to do some bridge work to cover it.

And always remember, if you send it in an email, it will probably end up on the front page of the New York Times.

12. Conference calls: Technology also gives a tool that helps teams of people talk who are geographically separated. This tool is the conference call.

Conference calls are excellent opportunities to build team cohesion, brief new ideas and concepts, provide information to support change, conduct training and many other activities. As such, they are invaluable tools for leaders to use. The downside of conference calls is the no-agenda call.

A conference call must be focused on a defined need. If there is no need, don't have a conference call. Scheduling regular conference calls can be more of a negative event than a positive event, simply because there may not be enough on the agenda to justify the time commitment by everyone attending.

Be careful in your use of the conference call. Ensure there is a real need. Have a real agenda. Manage the call to keep it focused and on track. Limit the time, and once the purpose of the call is complete, end the call.

13. Agendas: Since I mentioned it above, let me reinterate something. No meetings, except an urgent last minute meeting, should be conducted without an agenda. Meetings without agendas are unfocused, unprepared, rambling events that do not support effective execution.

Agendas should be written up, with topics, responsible individuals for each topic and time allocation for each topic. Someone should be designated as a time-keeper to keep the meeting on track and on time. Schedule some time at the end of the meeting for follow-up in case the initial time allotted is insufficient.

If a topic truly needs much more time than in your agenda, schedule a separate meeting to discuss this topic.

Agendas should be provided to each participant before the meeting, if at all possible, so they can come to the meeting prepared to discuss the topics of the meeting. If no one is aware of the topics and is not prepared, it is a basic waste of time.

For regular meetings, like staff meetings, there should be a written agenda. Just because it is a regular weekly meeting does not mean people should not know the topics or be prepared for discussion.

Agendas are important for organizing people's thoughts and focusing their energy. Use them. It avoids wasting time.

14. Time management and prioritization: Not enough can be written about how we manage our time. I have attended many different courses over the years, and the concepts in most of them make a lot of sense and work effectively.

I would encourage anyone to attend some time management or prioritization course(s). It is important to learn how to manage the only true resource you possess—your time.

Also, read books about the subject and take the time to really get into it to learn how to schedule effectively, utilize tools, like calendars and to do lists. You will only be better off as you learn more about how to manage and lead yourself, as a prelude or companion to learning to manage and lead others.

Learning the concepts and ideas from many sources is what helps us blend them into a cohesive pattern of behavior for our self. Once you have learned effective time management and prioritization, you can focus on more important things instead of being bogged down in having so much to do.

15. Counseling: Counseling is tough. Counseling makes you get out of your skin and get into someone else's. The work of counseling is squarely on your shoulders. You have to establish the communication tone, mood, atmosphere, subject matter, ideas and questions and prod the process along at a pace—not too fast or too slow—that meets the needs of the person you are counseling.

It is a difficult job. And the success of your team depends on your ability. So not only do you carry the weight of responsibility for the individual into the counseling session, you carry the weight of the responsibility for the team and your own performance into it.

On the other hand, counseling is fun. You get an opportunity to truly learn about someone and establish a bond of trust with them. This is not something that happens to us everyday, so take full advantage of it and build some relationships that will last.

16. Discipline: Discipline is a two fold topic. There is self discipline and disciplining others.

- Self discipline is critical to provide you the means to stick to your plans and goals as you work for self improvement. If you are not self disciplined, you will never be able to stay on task. Staying on task is a critical skill that enables you to keep your energy focused on getting it done, regardless of how tough or boring a task is.

- Disciplining others is also critical, in that you must balance the need for the participation of the work of a person with the need to change the behavior of that person. Discipline that is perceived as dead end will be rewarded with even worse performance. Finding the right balance, even if someone is not improving, is tough. But you have to try and you have to try with full intent of ensuring the disciplined person believes you are truly trying to help them. Employment becomes a simple choice for that person—either they will try and respond positively or they will not and seek their success elsewhere. But you must always be able to know you did your best.

17. Bonus Programs: Many people are paid a salary and some type of bonus or commission for performance. Even base salaries can be influenced in an annual performance review to determine who should get how much of an increase.

It is imperative that whatever the program you are part of, the program itself be perceived as fair by the ones who are evaluated through it. Like the comment on compensation issues above, if it is not perceived to be fair, it is not fair. It's as simple as that. People perceive their reality and to them, that is reality. For this reason, it is critical to ensure any changes to people's paychecks are accepted by all.

- In annual reviews, collect feedback from as many sources as you can to adequately evaluate performance. This can be metric measurement data, supervisory evaluative data, and peer and even subordinate evaluation data. All of these are thrown into the mix to give you the best numerical value you can associate for the person concerned, and the best comparative data to determine ranking and pay decisions.

- In quarterly bonus programs, use cumulative metric measurement data, as well as supervisory feedback to associate a numerical value to the person concerned. Don't use other feedback on quarterly bonus programs, as this provides for a cumbersome and continuously subjective evaluation that is not motivational for many people. The key to quarterly bonus programs is to reward business performance. Sticking to this will ensure your program rewards the behaviors all need to demonstrate and execute to insure your business maintains high performance.

- In commission programs, only use metric measurement data, such as individual product sales, team sales, market sales, etc. Data that is derived purely from actual performance metrics.

As you can see, the annual review is the most ambitious and all encompassing. This is because the salary increase provided based upon it is the longest lasting fixed personnel cost we have. Quarterly bonus and commission bonuses are derived basically from revenue generation, so are temporary and offset by revenue increases.

Bonus programs are critical to motivate people to perform. But remember, motivation is a two way street. You must ensure you are motivating positively and not negatively.

18. Working for Someone Younger Than Yourself: I have had the pleasure of working for people younger than me several times. I personally find it interesting, because our expectations are different. I know that sometimes these younger peo-

ple are more stressed than I, because of the experience and background I have, plus the uncomfortable feeling of having an older person working for them.

I believe the primary reason I have not had any difficulty working for younger people is that I understand they are in their position because of selection. They may have been with the company a long time, they may have better education, they may be the owners daughter–but whatever the reason, they were selected for their position, so the least they deserve from me is my best effort and good attitude.

I believe that is the secret, plus a good discussion about expectations. Whoever the boss is, they deserve the best performance you have. Sure, they look at things differently than you do, but that is irrelevant. As long as you are able to express your perspective in a positive manner, let them choose what they will. That is their prerogative as the supervisor. Your job is to support them to the best of your ability.

If you are so focused on the age gap and differences, you will not give them your best. Is that what you would expect from someone working for you? Of course not. In this case, you have the problem, not the younger supervisor.

19. Supervising Someone Older Than Yourself: I have also had the experience of supervising someone older than me. My experience, again, was positive. And again, I believe it was because I did not treat them any different, and we discussed expectations for their performance so we had a clear understanding of the working relationship.

It is interesting to supervise someone older. They have more experience. It may not be specific to your business, but they have had a longer time in which to grow and understand concepts.

They may have more experience in the business. In this case it is a tough balancing act, because you are the person charged with leading, but you now have someone on the team with more experience in your line of work than you. How do you effectively deal with this?

The best option is to bring them fully into the team. Treat them as equal. Give them responsibility for certain tasks or operations that show you are sharing the load with them. Ask them questions about why they do certain things. Show interest, listen and learn.

Discuss expectations and responsibilities. You can still let them know you are the decision maker while giving them a lot of room to maneuver–after all, whatever they do is still your responsibility and you still get credit for their success or failure. Talk about this with them.

The biggest single item is to talk. Talk openly, no hidden agendas, and establish a relationship with them. Give them the opportunity to demonstrate your trust in them. Or give them enough rope to show their true colors.

Also, talk with your leader regularly about what you are doing, so they are not surprised and support your actions. But never feel threatened. You are not in a position to lose your job to someone who is older and more experienced unless you screw it up. So do your job right, learn and grow and perform.

<u>20. Bringing Someone In From Another Organization–Not An Entry Level Employee:</u> When you hire an experienced person to join your team, you hire their skill, knowledge and experience. You also hire their expectations and process bias.

These are good and bad for the team. If they have a good work ethic, positive attitude and solid experience, it is totally good. If they do not, well, why did you hire them?

It is important that you allow the new team member time to adapt to the way your team behaves. It is equally important that you ask the new team member to provide you feedback on possible ways the team could improve. And then listen.

You find value in people before you bring them into your team. Once you bring them in, you have to fully utilize their strengths. *If you stifle them because of the way you do business, you do not use the strengths they possess fully. Then why did you hire them?*

Ask yourself what you need before you hire.

- Do you see that your team needs a boost in some area?

- Is there an area that is weak?

- Would external talent fill the gap?

- What exactly does the perspective new member bring to the table?

- Do they have several strengths that will give you what you need?

- Do they have strengths that will not be used?

- Do you have processes that will stifle their strengths?

- Are they decision makers and you only want their technical knowledge?

You truly must dig into this before you hire from the outside, because once you hire them they are on your team. Once someone is on your team, you have an obligation to develop and lead them. If you are bringing them into a situation in which they will not be fully successful, you are not taking care of your employee. *Why did you hire them?*

Bringing someone in from outside your organization is truly an opportunity to expand the skill and performance base of your team. My only caution is that you must know what you need before you advertise, and you must ensure you can accommodate both the needed skill of the new person as well as the other strengths the person has, so they can feel challenged and successful on your team.

21. Taking Over A New Team: There is a process to taking over a new team. There are two processes, actually.

- Process 1. The first one involves taking over a team with specific direction from leadership to go in and clean house. In this case, the only option is to adopt the demeanor of toughness and go in to evaluate who to get rid of and get rid of them. Secondary is the rebuilding effort to establish a new team dynamic.

- Process 2. The second one involves taking over a team with the action of engaging the team. In this process you go in with a learning attitude, being open and trusting while evaluating where strengths and opportunities lay. You follow this with conversation to stimulate the team to find solutions to problems and establish yourself from within the team as the team leader. This is the most effective manner in which to take control of a team.

In any event, you must be aware of the group dynamics in place when you are placed in charge of an existing team. They have history together and shared expectations. Their places are set, their paths are laid. If you come into a team such as this and do not work to build trust with them so as to become part of the team, you will eventually fail the team.

It is a process. Be non-judgmental. Be open-minded. Be prepared to accept their ideas and suggestions on what needs to be done. Don't be combative. Choose your areas to make change occur in non-threatening areas in non-threatening ways. Help them see that the direction is good and that they are valued.

After you have taken the time to establish this level of trust with a team, you can do anything. You can lead them where you believe they need to be and they will actively participate and follow. But you have to establish trust and competency and gain respect first.

There are a few steps I believe you must always follow whenever you are put in a leadership position with a new team. These are also steps you should follow in your normal working life as both a leader and follower to ensure you keep abreast of needs and change management.

1.   Observe—spend time observing who does what when and why and how, the results, needs and interwoven nature of all the activity and processes that takes place.

2.   Learn—take the time to learn from your observations so you will be able to intelligently discuss potential change options from a position of insider, not outsider.

3.   Understand—always take the time to understand the motivations of the people within the organization. These are the folks who do the work and generate the results. What do they expect, need and want to feel valued and successful?

4.   Reflect—take the time to reflect on your observations, what you have learned and the understanding of the human element. Only after truly getting into people's shoes, visualizing how they do what they do, where, working conditions, current expectations, performance levels, training needs, etc., can you begin to believe you have a grasp of the depth of your position.

5.   Act—take action at the right time in the right way.

These are the building blocks for success. These are the things that enable you to fully understand the biggest side of success–the internal nature of what success should or could look like for the people inside your organization.

22. Facilitating: There is a way to properly facilitate a team or group meeting, and there is a way to really screw it up. It is easy to do the latter, and more difficult to do the former.

• The wrong way to facilitate a team or group meeting is to get started late without a clear objective, allow rambling to occur, provide no fundamental process and allow the process to be variable. These will kill any good facilitation.

- The right way to facilitate a meeting is to

  - Be fully prepared before the meeting starts.
  - Start on time.
  - Have an agenda (that you stick too).
  - Have a recorder designated to document.
  - Have someone designated as time keeper to keep to the agenda.
  - Provide a solid, understandable visualization of the process the participants will be part of.
  - Pick a subject that is valid and quantifiable. If you pick a subject that is too big, it overwhelms and is unworkable.
  - Manage the conversation towards the goal.
  - Brainstorm ideas, not minutia.
  - Keep the process focused.
  - Keep people focused on the current task to prevent wandering.
  - Encourage participation.
  - Don't value out someone's idea or thought.
  - Keep focused and pushing for results.
  - Keep it friendly but professional.

23. The "But" Sandwich: One of the most ill used communication skills is the but sandwich. The problem with the but sandwich, is that it is so easy and natural to do. Here's an example.

"Sam said, "Sally, you performed that (activity) really well today. But your (skill or activity) stills lacks clarity. Still, your performance is really good."

What will Sally remember from this conversation? That her (skill or activity) still lacks clarity. She will probably not remember the two positives, because she will hear the but.

In addition, if Sam does this very often, Sally will come to expect that he uses the but sandwich not as a form of positive or true feedback, but as a way to mention the negative aspects of her performance.

How do you avoid the but sandwich? Give praise for work well done. Period. Stop. Don't continue. Then, at a later time, bring up the subject separately of an opportunity for improvement, after which you mention something positive.

In this way, Sally would hear praise for her work and be proud of it. Later on, she would hear a conversation about an area she could improve with positive encouragement. This fully supports her attitude, confidence and performance.

Give praise. Provide coaching. Do not try and do both at the same time. That is a but sandwich, but people only remember the but and not the praise.

24. "Happy to Glad": One of the most demotivating process applications a leader can implement is the "Happy to Glad" process.

What do I mean by happy to glad? It is simply to always make small changes to the documents people who work for you have completed.

This is not to be confused with a major editorial refocus, or a process/setup in which fundamental flaws are evident and must be corrected. Rather, this is when someone writes, for example, "We should evaluate this situation before moving forward," and the leader changes it to, "Let's evaluate this situation before we move forward." This change has no real substance, but effectively tells whoever submits documents to the leader that they can never write effectively, because the leader always finds something to change.

This is the happy to glad process. Telling someone they are not good enough by constantly changing small things slows down the process and demotivates the staff.

I have seen situations in which the leader kept sending a document back for changes to the point where it eventually was approved in virtually the same wording as the original submission. It is silly, wastes time, impedes good coordination, and reduces ownership and responsible performance, to change everything your staff does, just so you can say you made a change.

They know your changes are silly. Ultimately, the happy to glad changer is the one who has the poorest communication skill and lowest self esteem.

So let people write and communicate how they can. Provide suggestions and support, but if there is not a major flaw, let their communication go through as they wrote it. They will become more responsible, knowing their own writing is being used, and you will see them improve their ability over time.

25. Quality Improvement: There is always some current "quality improvement" platform making the rounds. Over the past several years, there have been a number of them, to include ISO, TQM, and 6 Sigma to name just a few. There are phrases like "win-win", "metric management", "data is friendly" and others that are used as slogans to support these and other platforms.

I call these platforms rather than programs, because all of these processes attempt to accomplish a similar purpose–improve performance. It is that each one approaches this singular process with differing emphasis, differing tools and different terminology that make them different platforms.

All of them are good, valid platforms. However, the platform you use must match the needs of the organization you are in as well as the personality of the leadership that will implement it. And all organizations need different things at different times and phases of their maturity.

So before you can get to the point of choosing the type of quality management platform your organization will utilize, you have to do some work. There are numerous questions to be answered before choosing. A few of the types of questions you need to ask yourself are:

- What is quality?

- What is excellence?

- How do you quantify it?

- How much methodology should be part of the process of measuring improvement?

- What is improvement?

- How important is efficiency compared to energized or excited employees?

- How do you define or quantify the variances that determine success?

- What is more important, long term success or short term success?

- Is long term success another way to stay stale and methodical?

- Should short term success be instilled as the steps up but only as part of a longer success vision?

- What does my organization need?

- Where does it need it the most?

- Why improve?

- What will the culture of my team support?

- How will it be affected?

I believe business is personal. As with so many personal things, the first step to define or redefine business is to answer a simple question that an individual must answer as well: "What is our (my) measure of success?"

Determining success is critical in any personal or business enterprise. Otherwise, you do not know where you are, where you have been or where you are going—or why you want or need to get there. Simply put, defining success provides the benchmark from which to measure all activity and performance, just as the organizational structure provides the fulcrum from which to move the organization towards the goal.

This is a leadership issue. What is success for your organization?

- Is it to continuously increase stock value?

- Is it to continuously provide higher and higher dividends to shareholders?

- Are these realistic measurements of success?

- Are they the most important?

- Are they the most sustainable?

- Are they the ones that inspire your employees to deliver excellence each and every day?

- Are they the ones that will be motivational for the organization for the long haul?

It is important to provide value to shareholders. That is not arguable. Without people purchasing your stock, in a public company, it becomes more difficult to raise capital to move your company towards your goal.

But having a goal or a clear measure of your success is of an even greater need. Because without it, you simply raise capital to achieve short term goals that you think will support long term goals that you think will help keep the company afloat. Is that success?

As I said earlier, a public company has shareholders and boards; all companies have budget considerations, fiscal strategies, etc; all companies depend on customers, so success depends on marketing strategies, etc. In short, there are many, many aspects of an organization to consider before a truthful definition of success can be attained.

But you have to start somewhere, and the place to begin is to define success. Once you define success, you can build the strategies you need to achieve and sustain that success.

Please don't be confused with vision statements. This success definition is not the vision. A vision is where the organization is going. It is the motivational and inspirational statement that keeps all the actions of the team focused on achieving the long term goals of the organization.

In a supporting role to the vision of an organization, the success definition is how we tell if we are being successful in the actual execution of the vision on a daily basis. Are you creating processes within the team to support the vision based on validating and increasing the level of success of the team?

Here is where success management becomes quality management. Here is where defining efficiency and improvement must be matched with the development of the energy of success.

It is well and good to say you are going to increase efficiency or productivity by a certain percent within a certain period of time. But if the accomplishment of that goal reduces employee effectiveness through decreased moral and increased frustration with leadership, what has truly been gained? Perhaps you can boast of a short term improvement, but you have also potentially laid the foundation for long term deterioration within the team. Was that a value based decision?

It would be better to work with the team that has the improvement needs you have identified. Explain to them the performance implications of how they do what they do. Show them how a new model could look. Ask them to help find ways to increase productivity and decrease inefficiencies. Ask them for ideas. Engage them in the process. Listen. Maybe they see how the process can be improved to only part of what you believe needs to be achieved. Go with that. Get that improvement. Get that buy in. Let them feel they are valued. Let them receive the benefits of the improvement. Let them be positive about the way business is conducted in their organization.

After you have gotten them to this point, continue to work with them to see how further enhancements can positively impact the team, customers, product and financial results. Get them to help you achieve success. That is success.

There are tools that most people do not understand or use on a regular basis. If you can, learn them yourself. If you do not have the time or your time requirements prevent it, hire someone who can do this for you. It does not hurt to have data at your fingertips. Data is friendly. However, it is in the application of change in regards to the revelations provided by the data that is collected and analyzed that success is measured.

It is important to define processes. It is important to gather data so you can evaluate processes for effectiveness and efficiency. It is important to set goals and drive for improvement. It is important to keep costs to an absolute minimum while maximizing performance to yield the highest return on investment. It is important to be competitive in the marketplace. All of these are important. The process of building from a foundation of success is not designed to reduce the importance of any of these items.

It is important though to do things in a way as to derive energy from within the team in a positive manner. That does not mean that everything will always be positive or no mandatory change will ever occur.

But all of the items listed can be both accomplished and enhanced through active engagement within the team in a success based scenario.

# 14

## *Processes/Tools*

I have always preferred to develop my own measurement tools. No offense against the tools developed by others, but they are *their* tools. While it is required to annotate the final results of many evaluations using corporate or Human Resource developed and approved forms, the actual evaluation can still be done individually in your own manner.

The creation of your own evaluative tool ties back into one of the basic bricks of this book–ownership. If you create the evaluative tool, you own the results of the tool. If you create a tool that is flawed, the results you get will be flawed, hence the decisions you make will be flawed.

This is, for many people, reason to embrace and only use the tools provided by someone else. However, this is yet another example of a process or method that needs individual ownership and excellence in application. After all, as a follower and a leader, you are selecting and developing the future through all your actions. This is the first action and the most critical, so you should own it entirely.

Remember, you should always run your ideas past a human resource professional. You cannot risk wrongly applying process in a way that violates law. However, if your ideas are within the law, there is no reason not to proceed.

Human resource professionals prefer to have you only use the tools they provide. There are many reasons for this, but simply put, this is because they view trying to manage a multitude of tools as uncontrollable. The fact is, however, that they should not try and control the created evaluative tools–they must, however, control the premise for tool development and ensure your creations do not violate law. They can and should mandate the final evaluation documents for official and annual evaluations, etc, that are corporate in nature.

The guiding principal I have used for tool development is quite simple–it must be thorough, skill focused and applied evenly. For this reason I usually resort to an excel spreadsheet type evaluation tool where I can create the measurement tools based on my evaluation of the skills, level of importance, and other characteristics necessary for a person to be effective in the position (or to perform effectively in the position in the case of an assessment looking for strengths and opportunities) combined with a weighted evaluation tool.

The next step is to create a set of open ended questions or other evaluative items you will use in the assessment you are creating. The following is an example of the two primary types of information you need to effectively evaluate an individual's performance. You must evaluate knowledge and ability.

| Ability | | | | | |
|---|---|---|---|---|---|
| | | Unable To Perform Tasks | Performs Simple Tasks | Performs Moderately Complex Tasks | Performs Most Complex Tasks | Performs All Tasks |
| **K n o w l e d g e** | Does Not Understand Processes | 1 | 2 | 3 | 4 | 5 |
| | Can Explain Simple Processes | 2 | 3 | 4 | 5 | 6 |
| | Can Explain Moderately Complex Processes | 3 | 4 | 5 | 6 | 7 |
| | Can Explain Most Complex Processes | 4 | 5 | 6 | 7 | 8 |
| | Understand All Processes | 5 | 6 | 7 | 8 | 9 |

As you can see, the higher the knowledge and the higher the ability equates to a higher evaluative score. When you are developing your questions or statements, make sure you are either evaluating knowledge or ability.

For example, if you ask someone to tell you about a time when they successfully overcame a customer's objection, you cannot use that to evaluate their knowledge of overcoming objections. Rather use this as a means to evaluate the ability. For knowledge evaluation, ask questions that require discussion answer to effectively evaluate the knowledge of the individual.

Many people have an incredibly hard time creating open-ended questions. Instead of saying: tell me about a time when you provided excellent customer service, they say: have you provided excellent customer service? As you can see, the results of these two statement/questions are going to be wildly different. Lean always in the direction of getting someone to talk.

Make statements or questions open-ended to get people to speak. You not only get to evaluate the quality of their response to the actual question, but you can evaluate how they think on their feet, how they communicate, etc. It is much more informative, and after all, that is what you need–information! Start open-ended questions with:

- Tell me about a time ...

- Give me an example of ...

- Tell me how your would handle ...

The great thing about this is that you can take the answers they give and run with it to the deepest levels of their skill. Use their experience and understanding of their experience as a measurement of their ability and knowledge.

Once you have designed questions and expected outcomes, you need to have a scoring system in place. The above chart graphically demonstrates the relationship between knowledge and ability, and provides a very good reference for creating tools. However, for a practical evaluative reference, I have found the 1–4 evaluation to be the most effective.

In this process, the scoring is based on only four numbers. The meaning of these four numbers must be clarified before you ever ask a question, so you apply them evenly to all. The scoring is thus:

- 4–Provided multiple examples **and** demonstrated excellent knowledge.

- 3–Provided at least two examples **or** demonstrated very good knowledge.

- 2–Provided at least one example **or** demonstrated minimal knowledge.

- 1–Provided no examples **and** demonstrated poor or less knowledge.

Using this as a guide, you can evaluate the response to any question or situation and apply the same measurement standard.

Up to this point we have discussed the creation of an evaluative tool, the need to create questions that discover answers to either knowledge or ability, and a means to score each question. The next decision is to determine what each question is worth.

In any tool, you can only discover 100% of the value you seek. You cannot have more than 100%. You are looking to determine the value of each response to your targeted questions using a scale that is defined carefully and equates to 100%.

As an example, let's say you are interviewing some candidates for a position. You first evaluate the position and determine what is truly important. The next step is to define the questions you will utilize to determine the knowledge and ability of the individuals concerned. You already have a scoring scale, so now you must create a weighted evaluative tool.

The example below is very minimal in nature. I would expect to have at minimum of 10 specific areas to evaluate, and depending on the importance or complexity of the assessment, more. The most important column on this chart is the Weight column.

In this example, notice the total weight is 1.00, which equates to 100%. The determination was that the most important aspect of these questions was the ability of the individual to adopt leadership traits as needed in the situations faced. The least valued was a knowledge understanding of the difference between management and leadership.

| | Weight | Jane Doe | Score | John Doe | Score | Jane Smith | Score | John Smith | Score |
|---|---|---|---|---|---|---|---|---|---|
| What is the difference between management and leadership? | 0.15 | 4.00 | 0.60 | 3.00 | 0.45 | 2.00 | 0.30 | 2.00 | 0.30 |
| Tell me about your leadership style. | 0.20 | 3.00 | 0.60 | 3.00 | 0.60 | 3.00 | 0.60 | 3.00 | 0.60 |
| Describe times when you used other leadership styles than the one you just described. | 0.40 | 2.00 | 0.80 | 3.00 | 1.20 | 2.00 | 0.80 | 1.00 | 0.40 |
| An employee has been late twice - what do you do? | 0.25 | 4.00 | 1.00 | 2.00 | 0.50 | 3.00 | 0.75 | 3.00 | 0.75 |
| Totals | 1.00 | 13.00 | 3.00 | 11.00 | 2.75 | 10.00 | 2.45 | 9.00 | 2.05 |

In this instance, Jane Doe has scored the highest. In an actual interview, John might have gotten the position simply because he potentially provided the best examples to the most important question. However, taken cumulatively, Jane is the best choice.

Creating measurement tools along these lines ensure you see the entire picture being presented and not a small slice. Also, by evaluating each person with the identical process, you realize a very accurate evaluative result.

The following are discussions with more detail about specific assessments. However, as my perspective is that you should create your own evaluative tools, I will not provide you a concrete example for you to use.

## 1. Basic Development Process:

The steps to completing this process are simple, yet entail considerable effort. The steps are:

- *Pre-Hire Selection:* Attitude + Ability = Access

- It is critical to ensure this first and most important step is completed properly. Behavioral interview training provides a great tool for interviewing potential candidates to ensure the best candidate from the pool is selected. Selecting the wrong person at the very beginning of the process leads to frustration, tension and on most occasions, failure.

- A person's attitude is usually unchangeable. It is possible, through the skill and character development stages to shift someone's attitude, however the preponderance of evidence suggests that the attitude you see at the beginning is the attitude you will get on a daily basis. Be careful then, to discover what someone truly brings to the table. The old adage, "People are on their very best behavior at the interview" is usually correct as well. The attitude, demeanor, dress and skill you observe at the interview is the best you will ever see. Make sure this very best meets your needs.

- Technical skill or knowledge can be taught. However, there are some skills and abilities people should have before they are hired. For example, people should have good time or task management, organization and planning skills. These can be worked on or enhanced, but it is time consuming and difficult. It is not appropriate to teach subset fundamental skills on the job. Some abilities people need to learn and bring with them.

- *Assessment:* Complete an assessment of the individual concerned. This assessment must be comprehensive. You need to review their resume, their capabilities, communication skill, attitude, technical knowledge, work ethic and anything else you deem appropriate for the position. Make sure you use the same assessment process for all hires, as it will provide you a tool for evaluating progress against the same standard.

- *Develop the Plan:* The plan you develop will be in stages, to ensure you complete a thorough, long-term development process.

  - Stage 1, Initial Base Skill: This part of your plan should include the technical knowledge and skill required, initial communication skill development, and emphasis on character in doing the correct and right thing. Most of these, except the discussions of character, are go/no-go skill or knowledge check-offs you make as you observe the actions of the employee.

  - Stage 2, Performance Delivery: As the skills of stage 1 above begin to gel, the next stage commences. In this stage you are working to ensure the employee can apply their skills and knowledge to effectively executing the mission. The plan should address required performance and analysis tools.

This is the phase where the employee brings all their resources to the table to show they have the potential to positively affect change.

- Stage 3, Increased Responsibility: As performance execution begins to yield positive results, the next stage begins. In this stage you begin to pass heat for performance to the employee and give them increasing responsibility for that performance. Simultaneously, you are working to encourage the employee to energetically accept ownership as a tool for executing effective leadership.

- Stage 4, Full Ownership: This last stage of development is the critical transition for the employee. At this time you are literally "weaning" the employee from your cover, as you transition full ownership to the employee. This is the key step into full leadership—energized, positive and performing.

- *Execute the plan:* No plan is worth a doodle if it isn't effectively executed. This is your responsibility. The capabilities of your followers are a direct reflection of how well you execute this plan. If you get too busy with "stuff", you will get mediocre results. If you execute as well as you need your followers to execute their positions, you will get excellent results. Even the potential mediocre performer will be above average when provided a solid and well executed development plan. However, only the occasional stellar performer will be excellent if the plan is sloppy, haphazard or poorly executed. This is leadership's key role.

- *Evaluate/Follow-up:* No plan is perfect when it is first initiated. Therefore, it behooves you to constantly review the plan against performance and changes. The plan must be tweaked and progress constant.

Understand the items above will most likely not happen in a series. They will most likely occur simultaneously, because people who are hired or promoted usually begin some form of training or job responsibility right away. This is a very fluid and dynamic process, which is why it requires such attention by the leader to ensure the correct development occurs.

Not only is the follower engaged in a dynamic ramp up process to full capability to do the job, but the leader must ensure the ramp up is inclusive of the leadership dynamic sought. This fluidity is seen as chaos by many, which explains the biggest excuse people give for not taking the time to properly and correctly establish a process for success.

The reason for clarifying this process into steps is to give you the opportunity to break down the overall task into pieces. As the leader, you began your assessment phase during the interview. You will continue to assess the employee while she is in training, learning the new positions parameters, figuring out specific requirements and working to achieve satisfactory results. You will be implementing your plan for training and developing this employee while you are assessing overall leadership development needs.

The very nature of this dynamic process demands documentation and accountability for thoroughness. If you do not create a documented plan and follow up to ensure you are effectively completing the entire plan, you will not get the results you seek.

## 2. Communication Self Assessment

The ability to effectively communicate is critical. In this book, communication has been a key item throughout. In the early chapters I discussed the need to complete a communication assessment. How do you assess your own communication ability? That is where, again, process must intervene. There are several means to communicate and it is important to ask yourself a lot of questions within each category.

If you do not know the answer, do not assume you must be successful in that area. Rather, ask questions to determine specifically where you stand in relation to each area.

This is not a total list. It is a guide for you to use to develop your own checklist, so you can ensure you cover all the bases. Use this as a starting point for your communication assessment. Make sure you add items as you see fit to cover all the aspects of communication that are pertinent to your evaluation.

- Written Communication

  - What is your grammatical ability?

  - Can you write effectively?

  - Is your writing at the correct educational level?

  - How many publications have you completed?

  - Is it important for you to have published work in your new or future positions?

  - Have you submitted written documents to higher ups?

  - What type of feedback have you received from those documents about your actual writing skill?

  - Are your written communications, such as email, misunderstood?

- Have you demonstrated clearly that you can write in an easy to understand manner?
- Is your writing style and skill developed enough for all your current and future positions?

- Oral Communication
  - What is your speaking ability?
  - Are you empathetic?
  - Is your interpersonal communication skill developed enough to enable you to succeed at your current or future levels?
  - Are you able to effectively speak in front of a team?
  - Do you effectively transfer meaning in your oral communication?
  - Have you spoken under pressure?
  - How well do you speak under pressure?
  - Is your oral communication always proper?

- Visual Communication
  - Is creation of visual communication part of your responsibility?
  - Have you learned and can you effectively utilize visual presentation software?

- Physical Communication
  - Does your body language match your words?
  - Do your words match your body language?
  - Are you constantly evaluating your perception to ensure your physical communication is correct and proper?

These are questions you need to ask yourself. Be honest. Be tough. If you do not know the answer to a particular question, go ask for feedback.

Once you have completed this process, you should know if you have the skills necessary for success in the position or if there are areas where you need improvement. Next—take action.

## 3. Initial Assessment and Development of New Employee

*General:* The purpose of this document is to provide a starting point for development of an effective assessment and development tool for new employees, whether new to the team or promoted to a new position. Remember, there are as many different tools as there are managers. I do not recommend you use anything other than the tool you design. This will give you the assurance that you are thoroughly completing this task. The tool development process is not complex, but it provides you additional insight into the assessment and development process by forcing you to make evaluative decisions. I have found a program like Microsoft Excel to be a very good tool for building this type of document. It enables you to track percentage of improvement, average level of knowledge or task completion, etc., that other programs do not offer. Using prepared tools can be effective and still accomplish the task; however, your own tool developed within certain established criteria will give you the most assurance of success. I would expect you to build a basic tool for each position and edit this as necessary over time.

*Process:* The process for developing a tool is relatively strait-forward. It requires you, as the leader; to thoroughly know the position you are entering someone into. For some people, this step is an eye opener, as they do not truly know the many items a position is required to perform, instead looking at the overall totality of the position. Use this as a tool for your own edification as well as a tool to ensure your followers receive the best possible and most thorough development process possible. The results down the line will be worth the investment in your time and detail. As you work through development of your tool, ensure you identify everything you can think of and then ask someone in a similar position and your Human Resource team to review to ensure you have not missed anything. This will ensure 100% knowledge and skill coverage for all items.

1. Document specific skills necessary to successfully function in this position. These skills must include all skills relative and appropriate for the position. These skills can include technology familiarity, software and computer skill, verbal and written communication skill, equipment, process or other job specific skills, and other requirements as you see fit.

2. Document all of the specific job tasks for the new position. Using the skill set data above; list all the tasks the position completes. Think about not only specific responsibilities, but also cross-functional coordination that helps ensure a smooth

workflow, informal as well as formal line of communication requirements, people development skills and any other items you see fit.

3. Document the specific job knowledge required to accomplish the tasks for the position. Knowledge differs from tasks in that tasks are applied knowledge. Knowledge requirements exceed task requirements because a greater knowledge base is required to complete tasks effectively. There must be an understanding of cause and effect from task completion or failure. For example, the knowledge of the impact on task completion to the team, company or another performance unit would be a knowledge item, not necessarily a task item.

4. Document the specific levels of responsibility/accountability for the position. At the entry level, the greater emphasis will be on learning and development. The next level will be increased responsibility for performance. Lastly will be full accountability. As you create this assessment/development tool, ensure you specify the various levels of responsibility/accountability and evaluate as such.

5. Develop a rating scale with clear levels of understanding. For example, a go/no-go scale is valid for tasks. Simply put, either the person can effectively perform the task or she cannot. Three tiered scales are also very accurate: agree/disagree/not applicable. Five tiered scales are also applicable and very accurate: strongly agree, agree, neither agree nor disagree, disagree, strongly disagree. Lastly, scales from one to five are accurate: 1–completely unacceptable or incapable, 2–less than average acceptability or competence, 3–average performance or competency, 4–above average acceptability or competence, 5–exceptional acceptability or high competence. Any of these scales can give you excellent evaluative tools. It is important to specify exactly what you mean in the evaluation process. If, for example, you used the one to five scale, provide a solid and complete word picture of what each rating means, so the evaluator and evaluatee are on the same wave length. As part of this process will be self-assessment based, it is critical that all evaluations adhere to the same understanding.

## 4. Skill Development Matrix:

The following skills and behavior characteristics are those that I have found to be the most important in development of leadership. They begin with the followership skill of providing solutions and end with the leadership skill of visionary.

I have found all of these to be valid and useful in striving for self-development and in designing coaching scenarios for employees. Please use them as you see fit for ideas on which skills your employees or yourself need in order to move to the next higher level.

| Specific Skill | Macro Focus Area | Chapter |
|---|---|---|
| Visionary | Leadership | Visionary |
| Inspires | Leadership | Visionary |
| Shares Credit | Leadership | Visionary |
| Trusting | Leadership | Visionary |
| Influences Others | Leadership | Visionary |
| Public Speaking | Leadership | Visionary |
| Sociable | Leadership | Visionary |
| Sets Goals | Leadership | Engaged |
| Manages Organizations | Leadership | Engaged |
| Develops Evaluation Strategy | Leadership | Engaged |
| Facilitating group discussion | Leadership | Engaged |
| Analyzing | Leadership | Engaged |
| Defines Needs | Leadership | Engaged |
| Creates meaningful work | Leadership | Reinforce, Develop, Coach, Mentor |
| Conflict management | Leadership | Reinforce, Develop, Coach, Mentor |
| Team Oriented | Leadership | Reinforce, Develop, Coach, Mentor |
| Coach | Leadership | Reinforce, Develop, Coach, Mentor |
| Persuading | Leadership | Reinforce, Develop, Coach, Mentor |
| Communicator | Leadership | Reinforce, Develop, Coach, Mentor |
| Tolerant | Leadership | Reinforce, Develop, Coach, Mentor |
| Sense of humor | Leadership | Reinforce, Develop, Coach, Mentor |
| Mentoring | Leadership | Reinforce, Develop, Coach, Mentor |
| Forecasting, predicting | Leadership | Situational Awareness/Leadership |
| Exhibits Sound Judgment | Leadership | Situational Awareness/Leadership |
| Observes People/Processes | Leadership | Situational Awareness/Leadership |
| Tough | Leadership | Situational Awareness/Leadership |
| Confronts | Leadership | Situational Awareness/Leadership |
| Delegates | Leadership | Situational Awareness/Leadership |
| Prioritizes | Leadership | Situational Awareness/Leadership |
| Empathetic | Leadership | Situational Awareness/Leadership |
| Achieves Goals | Leadership | Situational Awareness/Leadership |
| Risk Taker | Ownership | Transcendence |
| Accepts Responsibility | Ownership | Transcendence |
| Decision Maker | Ownership | Transcendence |
| Promotes Change | Ownership | Transcendence |
| Active Involvement | Ownership | Transcendence |
| Enforces Policy | Ownership | Transcendence |
| Competitive | Ownership | Transcendence |
| Implements Decisions | Ownership | Transcendence |
| Strategic In Planning | Ownership | Sense of Value & Purpose |
| Sense of Purpose | Ownership | Sense of Value & Purpose |
| Planning | Ownership | Sense of Value & Purpose |

| Maintains Control Under Stress | Ownership | Sense of Value & Purpose |
|---|---|---|
| Thorough | Ownership | Sense of Value & Purpose |
| Responsible | Ownership | Sense of Value & Purpose |
| Mature | Ownership | Sense of Value & Purpose |
| Reads | Ownership | Sense of Value & Purpose |
| Consulting | Ownership | Process Orientation |
| Program Administration | Ownership | Process Orientation |
| Inspects | Ownership | Process Orientation |
| Project Management | Ownership | Process Orientation |
| Evaluating | Ownership | Process Orientation |
| Negotiating | Ownership | Process Orientation |
| Financial Management | Ownership | Developing Ownership |
| Results oriented | Ownership | Developing Ownership |
| Ambitious | Ownership | Developing Ownership |
| Dependable | Ownership | Developing Ownership |
| Handling Details | Ownership | Developing Ownership |
| Managing time | Ownership | Developing Ownership |
| Quality Oriented | Ownership | Developing Ownership |
| Efficiency | Ownership | Developing Ownership |
| Punctual | Ownership | Developing Ownership |
| Tactical In Action | Followership | Execution Oriented |
| Execution Oriented | Followership | Execution Oriented |
| Directing Work | Followership | Execution Oriented |
| Motivated | Followership | Execution Oriented |
| Competent | Followership | Execution Oriented |
| Concise | Followership | Execution Oriented |
| Detail Oriented | Followership | Execution Oriented |
| Customer Oriented | Followership | Execution Oriented |
| Perform | Followership | Execution Oriented |
| Versatile | Followership | Personal Characteristic |
| Research | Followership | Personal Characteristic |
| Enthusiastic | Followership | Personal Characteristic |
| Encouraging | Followership | Personal Characteristic |
| Flexible | Followership | Personal Characteristic |
| Organized | Followership | Personal Characteristic |
| Honest | Followership | Personal Characteristic |
| Integrity | Followership | Personal Characteristic |
| Tactful | Followership | Personal Characteristic |
| Multi-Tasker | Followership | Personal Characteristic |
| Reliable | Followership | Personal Characteristic |
| Adaptable | Followership | Personal Characteristic |
| Intelligent | Followership | Personal Characteristic |
| Endurance | Followership | Personal Characteristic |
| Develop Rapport | Followership | Communication |
| Listens | Followership | Communication |

| Teaches | Followership | Communication |
|---|---|---|
| Disseminating Information | Followership | Communication |
| Disciplines, As Needed | Followership | Courage |
| Counseling | Followership | Courage |
| Non-Biased | Followership | Courage |
| Provides Solutions | Followership | Courage |

<u>5. Progression:</u> There is a natural progression of skill development. This begins with the new hire or apprentice level and culminates in leadership. Not everyone makes the journey. Many people move to the worker level and remain there. Some move to the supervisor level and remain there. These individuals can still demonstrate ownership and leadership attributes, however, they do not move beyond this level to hold accountability for a larger team.

There are also many who become managers. They too can demonstrate higher levels of followership and ownership while displaying good leadership attributes. However, they may not risk taking full accountability and stepping up to a true leadership position.

Lastly, of course, are those who embrace accountability through ownership, learn that the skills of followership demonstrate leadership traits, and begin to feel the sense of value and purpose a leader feels. For these individuals, there is no limit to their potential.

<u>6. Where do you spend your time?</u> This is one of the most important time and task management tools I know. Since the only thing you truly possess is your time, where you spend it becomes critical.

There are several models you can use, but essentially, the more important and urgent a task is, the more attention you should spend on it.

This is not the case for many people during many work days. A lot of people spend their time doing urgent things, but not important things. This is where "fire fighting" comes in. How many times do you respond to something someone else said was needed right away? How often do you spend time reacting to something that needs a response quickly? These are the fire fighting events that take away the day.

It is much more important to do the things you know are urgent AND important. How often can you take time to devote to planning? Many people do not spend time planning, but planning and organizing are two of the most important things you can do. Add this to planning business changes, response to threats, means or ways to market to take advantage of an opportunity, and you are in the urgent and important square.

It should be said that anything that fits in the low importance and low urgency square should be eliminated. Likewise, if you only focus on important things but don't consider whether they are urgent or not, you are potentially day dreaming. Keep aware of how you are spending your time. Manage your time to ensure you are leading yourself into the urgent and important square. This is where ownership and leadership and the most necessary.

# *Summary*

It makes sense to provide a pathway for leadership development. It makes sense to provide the time, attention and resources needed to ensure this process is the most effective it can possibly be. It especially makes sense to create and implement effective development processes for the first transition from being a working individual to a supervisory individual. After all, these individuals will be the future leaders of your organization. Don't you think you should create the best possible replacements?

The question that begs to be answered is this: "If leadership is the goal, what are the steps to get there?" It is a valid question, and one that I set out to answer, from my perspective, in this book.

Growing leadership is a process. It is an individual process. It is a group dynamic process. It is an organizational process. Regardless of how you look at it, it is a process. The performance I have seen in several organizations is that while it is a process that receives a lot of attention, it is not a process that receives a lot of resources.

That is not to say we do not throw money at it. But money is not the key. The key is the personal time commitment and relationships that influence, coach and grow people into effective leaders. The key is creating and effectively managing through the developmental chaos that exists.

We expect people to learn. We expect people to take on a new position and want to be successful to the point that we expect them to work hard at learning leadership.

We give people some discussion and conversation. We provide some seminars and meetings. But we don't put them into a situation where they receive the type of coaching and personal development that is necessary for truly effective leadership growth.

This is not the fault of any specific organization or any values of those organizations. Because at their core, all people know that they need people to lead. We all need leaders for our teams. We need leaders for our business units, organizations—you name it, we need a leader for it.

One problem is that we accept managers instead of demanding leaders. We place someone in a position as manager and expect they will learn leadership skill. It just doesn't work that way. People will only learn what you teach them.

As you have followed in this book, I have laid out a process that follows.

- The first thing we need to do is actively ensure our new managers and supervisors understand that they need to begin by mimicking the behaviors of leaders.

- Then, as they do this and become more competent in all their technical tasks and leadership tasks, we begin increasing their responsibility without full accountability.

- As they grow in competence and truly begin to take on the responsibility, we shift them into ownership and accept accountability for their performance.

- As this ownership energizes them and they continue to grow, they shift into leadership through their sense of value and purpose. It is a simple process.

The individual who uses this process from within can enhance the experience they have in leadership development because they begin to control their own destiny. They can ask the tough questions and get their leaders to provide them the support they need–even if the leader is unaware they need it. That is courage.

So much of how we do what we do is not documented. Learning leadership is not a documented or clear process. Only leaders understand what needs to be taught. But leaders are usually too engaged in their own processes to take the time to document it.

Also, many leaders are part of organizations that are concerned about fiscal constraints and just do not have the resources to devote to effective development processes. We get by and send people to seminars and classes now and then.

We must change how we grow leadership. It only makes sense. I know the processes in this book work because I have taken the time to use them and seen the results. Use them. Make growing leaders sensible. After all, it is the right thing to do.

Lastly, being the best you can be, in regards to developing your character and ability, is the right thing to do for personal development and growth. We all get older. Not everyone gets older while experiencing the depth of value that can be found from true ownership of their person, their time and their relationships. You have that power.

Use this power in the proactive development of leadership within yourself. Develop your character in the highest manner. Be the best you can be doing the best you can do. Don't sell yourself short. Lead.

# Bibliography

This is only a sample of the authors and books that individuals interested in growing leadership should read. Most of the authors below have more books than the one or two listed. It would be a very good idea to take some time, as you read these books, to find other titles from these authors and to further expand your reading list to titles and authors not listed below.

I have also found the CD recordings of many of these books to be very helpful. Listening to the words sometimes provides a different visualization of the concepts and enhances the learning experience.

Lundin, Stephen C., Harry Paul, and John Christensen. *FISH!* New York: Hyperion, 2000

Worman, David. *Motivating Without Money.* Omaha: Business By Phone Inc., 2003

Byham, William C., Jeff Cox. *Zapp! The Lightning of Empowerment.* 2nd Ed. New York: Ballentine, 1998

Blanchard, Kenneth, Spencer Johnson. *The One Minute Manager.* New York: Berekley, 1982

Johnson, Spencer, Kenneth Blanchard. *Who Moved My Cheese?* New York: Penguin, 1998

Fournies, Ferdinand F. *Coaching for Improved Work Performance.* New York: McGraw-Hill, 2000

Drucker, Peter F. *Managing In the Next Society.* New York: St. Martin's, 2002

Blanchard, Kenneth. *Leadership and the One Minute Manager.* New York: William Morrow, 1985

Robbins, Stephen P., Phillip L. Hunsaker. *Training In Interpersonal Skills, Tips For Managing People at Work.* 2nd Ed. Upper Saddle River: Simon & Schuster, 1996

Covey, Stephen R. *7 Habits of Highly Effective People.* New York: Simon & Schuster, 1989

Loehr, Jim, Tony Schwartz. *The Power of Full Engagement.* New York: Simon & Schuster, 2003

Blanchard, Kenneth. *Raving Fans.* New York: William Morrow, 1993

McGraw, Phillip C. *Self Matters, Creating Your Life from the Inside Out.* New York: Simon & Schuster, 2001

Bossidy, Larry, Ram Charin. *Execution, The Discipline of Getting Things Done.* New York: Random House, 2002

Collins, Jim. *Good To Great.* New York: Harper Collins, 2001

Drucker, Peter F., Joseph A. Maciariello. *The Daily Drucker.* New York: Harper Collins, 2004

Blanchard, Kenneth, Thad Lacinak, Chuck Tompkins, Jim Ballard. *Whale Done!* New York: Simon & Schuster, 2002

Fast, Julius. *Body Language.* New York: MJF, 2002

Charan, Rom. *What The Customer Wants You To Know.* New York: Penguin, 2007

Covey, Stephen M. R., Rebecca R. Merrill. *The Speed of Trust.* New York: Simon & Schuster, 2006

978-0-595-50603-3
0-595-50603-8

Lightning Source UK Ltd.
Milton Keynes UK
19 August 2010

158664UK00003B/89/P